The
Technology
Revolution

Other books in the Turning Points series:

Turning | Points
IN WORLD HISTORY

The Technology Revolution

Clarice Swisher, *Book Editor*

Daniel Leone, *President*
Bonnie Szumski, *Publisher*
Scott Barbour, *Managing Editor*

GREENHAVEN PRESS
SAN DIEGO, CALIFORNIA

THOMSON
━━━━✦━━━ ™
GALE

Detroit • New York • San Diego • San Francisco
Boston • New Haven, Conn. • Waterville, Maine
London • Munich

Library of Congress Cataloging-in-Publication Data

The technology revolution / Clarice Swisher, book editor.
  p. cm. — (Turning points in world history)
  Includes bibliographical references and index.
  ISBN 0-7377-0931-6 (lib. bdg. : alk. paper)—
ISBN 0-7377-0930-8 (pbk. : alk. paper)
  1. Computers and civilization. 2. Computers. I. Swisher, Clarice, 1933– II. Turning points in world history (Greenhaven Press)

QA76.9.C66 T33 2002
303.48'34—dc21   2001054326

Copyright © 2002 by Greenhaven Press,
an imprint of The Gale Group
10911 Technology Place, San Diego, CA 92127

Printed in the U.S.A.

Contents

useful in the investment business as the market becomes more complex. AI can handle many variables, calculate rapidly, learn from mistakes, and make changes.

Chapter 2: Technology's Effects on Business and Industry

Chapter 3: Society in the Computer Age

distribution of pornography; in 1999, however, just over half of the states had laws specifically making pornography on the Internet illegal. The issue of "virtual" child pornography causes a more heated debate because it involves a free-speech issue.

Chapter 4: The Technology of the Future

Technology reduces the cost and time needed to fill a job. Gone are the days of paper résumés, data-based matches of applicant to job description, and searches on multiple websites. In the future an applicant will have a universal résumé, including a digital video. Companies seeking employees will have their own digital videos plus the software to match applicant to job quickly and inexpensively.

Five developing technologies will change innumerable services in the future. Broadband will provide services on one line. Wireless will provide the speed to make handsets more versatile. Software will be rented and downloaded, and digital cash will make shopping safer. With wireless appliances, new products can be inserted with ease.

Foreword

Certain past events stand out as pivotal, as having effects and outcomes that change the course of history. These events are often referred to as turning points. Historian Louis L. Snyder provides this useful definition:

> A turning point in history is an event, happening, or stage which thrusts the course of historical development into a different direction. By definition a turning point is a great event, but it is even more—a great event with the explosive impact of altering the trend of man's life on the planet.

History's turning points have taken many forms. Some were single, brief, and shattering events with immediate and obvious impact. The invasion of Britain by William the Conqueror in 1066, for example, swiftly transformed that land's political and social institutions and paved the way for the rise of the modern English nation. By contrast, other single events were deemed of minor significance when they occurred, only later recognized as turning points. The assassination of a little-known European nobleman, Archduke Franz Ferdinand, on June 28, 1914, in the Bosnian town of Sarajevo was such an event; only after it touched off a chain reaction of political-military crises that escalated into the global conflict known as World War I did the murder's true significance become evident.

Other crucial turning points occurred not in terms of a few hours, days, months, or even years, but instead as evolutionary developments spanning decades or even centuries. One of the most pivotal turning points in human history, for instance—the development of agriculture, which replaced nomadic hunter-gatherer societies with more permanent settlements—occurred over the course of many generations. Still other great turning points were neither events nor developments, but rather revolutionary new inventions and innovations that significantly altered social customs and ideas, military tactics, home life, the spread of knowledge, and the human condition in general. The developments of writing, gunpowder, the printing press, antibiotics, the electric light, atomic energy, television, and the computer, the last two of which have recently ushered in the world-altering information age, represent only some of these innovative turning points.

Each anthology in the Greenhaven Turning Points in World History series presents a group of essays chosen for their accessibility. The anthology's structure also enhances this accessibility. First, an introductory essay provides a general overview of the principal events and figures involved, placing the topic in its historical context. The essays that follow explore various aspects in more detail, some targeting political trends and consequences, others social, literary, cultural, and/or technological ramifications, and still others pivotal leaders and other influential figures. To aid the reader in choosing the material of immediate interest or need, each essay is introduced by a concise summary of the contributing writer's main themes and insights.

In addition, each volume contains extensive research tools, including a collection of excerpts from primary source documents pertaining to the historical events and figures under discussion. In the anthology on the French Revolution, for example, readers can examine the works of Rousseau, Voltaire, and other writers and thinkers whose championing of human rights helped fuel the French people's growing desire for liberty; the French *Declaration of the Rights of Man and Citizen*, presented to King Louis XVI by the French National Assembly on October 2, 1789; and eyewitness accounts of the attack on the royal palace and the horrors of the Reign of Terror. To guide students interested in pursuing further research on the subject, each volume features an extensive bibliography, which for easy access has been divided into separate sections by topic. Finally, a comprehensive index allows readers to scan and locate content efficiently. Each of the anthologies in the Greenhaven Turning Points in World History series provides students with a complete, detailed, and enlightening examination of a crucial historical watershed.

Introduction: The Technology Revolution and Its Social Effects

Computers have a profound effect on modern life. Most people today use a computer every day, even if they do not work with computers in their jobs; they use computers when they go to an ATM machine, use a CD player or VCR, or drive a car. At the beginning of a panel discussion sponsored by *Discover* magazine and the Disney Institute, "The Startling Future of Computers," Bran Ferron, the moderator, said,

> The computer age has been characterized as both the greatest wonder of technology and our worst nightmare. In only a few decades, these often mystifying machines have transformed our existence, easing daily tasks, taking over humdrum work, and making a lot of other machinery around us run more reliably and efficiently. Yet there is something in most people that does not love a computer. We remain suspicious of its power—and potential.[1]

These "mystifying machines" are at the heart of the revolution currently transforming modern life at a rapid pace. This transformation raises important issues: the extent to which computers have penetrated daily life, the rapid changes that have brought about this phenomena in just a few decades, the benefits and risks of this revolution, and predictions for the ongoing nature of computer technology.

Indeed, computers are faster, more powerful, and more widespread. Three categories of computers prevail today: mainframes and personal computers that run software; embedded chips that control machines, such as microwave ovens, automobile braking systems, telephones, and medical instruments; and the Internet, which is built on computer-controlled devices. Computer science teacher Sara Baase says, "Computer technology, many would agree, is the most significant new technology since the beginning of the Industrial Revolution."[2] During the eighteenth and nineteenth centuries, the Industrial Revolution in England disrupted an agricultural way of life and replaced it with an urban manufacturing society, displacing huge populations of people. In 1981 engineer Howard Rosenbrock thought that the computer phenomena would be different—not new but an intensification of familiar tendencies. In the article "A New Industrial Revolution?" he stated,

> We do not see microelectronics and computers and communication systems as bringing a new departure comparable to that which occurred in England. . . . To say that the next 20 years will see not a new beginning, but an intensification of old tendencies, is not to diminish the importance of the changes that will occur. These are likely to be faster and more extensive than anything in recent experience. . . . The problems we shall face will be not wholly new ones, but those with which we are familiar, though perhaps intensified and extended.[3]

Today we are too immersed in the ongoing changes to know if the computer has started a new beginning or has intensified old tendencies; time and history will provide that understanding.

Rapid Changes in a Short Time

It is clear that the computer revolution has occurred piecemeal in just a few decades. The first commercial, general-purpose computer was delivered to the U.S. Bureau of Census in 1951. By 1953 an estimated one hundred computers existed in the entire world. The first commercial supercomputer was developed and the first personal computers (PCs) were marketed during the late 1970s. The first video game was released in 1978. In 1989 the World Wide Web was invented as an information exchange for physicists, and in 1993 commercial providers could sell Internet connections to individuals, beginning the explosion of Internet use. By 1994 one in three American households had a PC, and a billion computer chips were produced each week. The number of transistors that can be placed on a chip has doubled about every eighteen months for more than three decades. Today

PCs and Internet access are commonplace, and big changes are coming. An April 2001 report in the *Economist* predicts,

> Unless they [computer companies] have all got it wrong, companies, consumers and computers will one day be able to choose exactly what they want from a huge cloud of electronic offerings, via the Internet. . . . There is no doubt that something big is happening in the computer industry—as big as the rise of the PC in the 1980s that turned hardware into a commodity and put software squarely at the center of the industry. Now it looks as though software will have to cede its throne to services delivered online.[4]

And yet as computers have gained in speed, power, and prevalence, their cost has dramatically dropped. Michael Rothchild, in "Beyond Repair: The Politics of the Machine Age Are Hopelessly Obsolete," says that since 1971 "the cost of computing has plunged 100 million-fold. That's like being able to buy a new Boeing 747 for the price of a large pizza."[5]

The Benefits for Manufacturing

As prices declined over the decades, factory managers took advantage of the benefits computers offered. Computer-aided tool design, machine control, process and materials planning, and robotics have made factory management more efficient and cost effective. Computerized machines can be reprogrammed quickly and easily to allow manufacturers to make products according to the customers' specifications. In "Flexible Manufacturing Systems," Gene Bylinsky with Alicia Hills Moore explain: "Different products can be made on the same line at will. General Electric, for instance, uses flexible automation to make 2000 different versions of its basic electric meter at its Somersworth, New Hampshire, plant with total output of more than a million meters a year."[6]

In *Computers and Society: Impact!* David O. Arnold explains how computers have revolutionized factory inventory, another way of saving money.

> The technique is called **just-in-time** manufacturing, or **JIT**. . . . With JIT, managers enter three sets of information into the computer: The parts needed for each product, the de-

mand for each product (based on orders received), and the time required to order and receive each part from a given supplier. Parts are then ordered so that they arrive *just in time* to be used in the manufacturing process.[7]

General Motor's seat-cover plant reduced its inventory from ten to three days with JIT.

The Benefits for Offices, Banks, and Retail Stores

Laptop computers and work stations in homes and offices have allowed workers to access information and carry on work tasks from many locations. Recent computer systems also make complex tasks that require flexibility faster and easier. In *Business @ the Speed of Thought*, Bill Gates describes how new computer technology assists business thinking to create a digital nervous system, an infrastructure that can operate with speed and flexibility. For example, companies need to vary their staffing with more or fewer workers, depending on demand. Gates explains, "The Web workstyle makes it possible to deal better with unpredictable demand. Because you have an intense need for a skill, and then you don't, for some areas you want flexible staffing to deal with peaks and valleys."[8]

When banks use computers to work more conveniently and flexibly, they usually decrease costs at the same time. Banks have been leaders in providing computer services, for example, by making account information instantly accessible, automatic transfer of funds possible, ATM machines conveniently located, and loans obtainable online. Electronic banking has allowed banks to cope with the increased demand for services while reducing the number of employees at the same time.

Like banks, retailer stores reduce costs when they use computers. Computers facilitate checkout with fast scanning devices and provide better inventory control by tracking sales and stock. Computers are also good for the environment because their use reduces waste paper. One department store chain reported saving a million dollars by keeping sales reports on the computer.

The Benefits in Medicine

Today computers benefit medicine in a multitude of ways. In hospitals, they handle billing and accounting; admissions, discharges, and transfers; and store medical records. Computers are embedded in image-monitoring machines and in technology that allows doctors to perform surgery by making tiny, rather than large, incisions.

New developments using wireless communication, video-conferencing, and telemedicine have become available recently. For example, doctors at the University of Maryland Medical Center and the Maryland School of Medicine in Baltimore "are the first in the nation to use video and computer technology to assess a stroke victim while the patient is in an ambulance. That could be critical, because a key clot-busting drug for stroke victims can only be given within three hours after symptoms begin."[9] Also using a multimedia computer with Internet and videoconferencing capabilities, doctors at the Harvard Medical School have designed Baby CareLink, a system to be installed in the home of parents whose low–birth weight baby has to remain in the hospital. The system allows parents to monitor their baby daily. Technologies like these potentially save lives and lower costs.

Moreover, computer-based technologies have provided medical services over long distances. Doctors in rural areas gain access to specialized diagnostic information and medical advice by consulting medical databases. Recently the British Broadcasting Company reported on complex technology that allowed a surgeon in one city to perform an operation on a patient in another city. A team of doctors stood by at the patient's side in case the technology failed, but they were not needed.

The *American Medical News* reported in April 2001 that most practicing physicians "believe computers have had a positive impact on medicine," but they were less enthusiastic about Internet-related business and clinical services. They believe "the Internet won't fully become a part of physician practices unless the Health Care Financing Administration or major health plans require its use for such services as claims processing."[10]

Computers Benefit Publishers

Computers have transformed the publishing industry. Today individuals using computers for desktop publishing produce professional-looking brochures and books at minimal cost. Small companies can publish limited editions of specialized books; in former times, the cost of setting up production was so time consuming and costly that companies could afford only titles with large runs. At large publishing companies, manuscripts are sent by e-mail, scanners reproduce pictures and type, and computers coordinate brightness and intensity of color. Dictionaries published on the Internet can be kept up to date annually or more often, as opposed to publishing a new edition only every decade or so. As a result of computers, the public enjoys books with more attractive design and interesting illustrations and books with more specialized and up-to-date material. Increasingly readers are finding published material available on the Internet.

Computers Aid Researchers

Computers and the Internet make new kinds of research possible and traditional kinds of research more efficient. The most obvious benefit is the ability to store masses of data on the computer and sort it quickly for easy use. An increasing number of materials are available online. For example, by 1995 the Library of Congress had digitized more than two hundred thousand items, including its American history collection with its many fragile items, and the library has made many more volumes available since. Major museums around the world have made works of art available on CD-ROM. Rare literary works are often available as never before. As Baase points out,

> The British Library owns the 11th century manuscript of *Beowulf*, studied by scholars from all over the world. Digitized images of the manuscript are now available to scholars on the Internet. The quality is so good that words erased by the original scribes, fire damage, and changes made in a 19th century restoration are visible.[11]

Online materials like these allow the researcher to save time and money and increase the quality and thoroughness of study.

Another kind of research uses satellites for environmental studies. The August 2001 issue of *Birder's World* reports on three projects that use satellites to track the movement and habits of tundra swans in the Atlantic Flyway, to follow peregrine falcon migration from sites in Virginia and Maryland, and to study the habits of ducks and Canada geese. These are long-term tracking projects to learn about the breeding grounds, the stopover locations, and survival rates of these species—projects impossible to research without computer technology.

Computers for Private Use

Individuals use computers in all varieties of private projects for education, enjoyment, and work. For example, students can study subjects their schools do not provide in the regular curriculum. In rural areas local school districts are often unable to offer specialized or advanced courses. Students can use programs that teach foreign languages and hear instruction spoken with correct pronunciation by native speakers. For enjoyment, individuals can form virtual communities and interact socially or join like-minded people from around the globe in discussion groups on thousands of topics. Composers, too, enjoy the convenience of computers in their work. For centuries they worked out compositions on instruments and laboriously wrote out the notes on music paper. Now they can play new compositions on an electronic keyboard, and the notes appear on a screen in standard musical notation, ready to print. An individual cyclist can train more efficiently with an eight-function computer that provides information on a display panel similar to those on watches; it has a clock, a stopwatch, gear ratio, cadence (pedal revolutions per minute), total miles, trip miles, speed, and average speed. Computers have indeed transformed the way people function in their private lives.

Computers Improve Public Service

The computer revolution has also greatly benefited society. Many public services have been improved and expanded with the use of new technology. A few examples illustrate this: Local communities provide better traffic control; journalists provide more accurate political polling; the federal government provides quick census analysis and efficient postal service all with the benefit of computers. Police can search databases for vehicle registration, fingerprints, and criminal records to help identify suspects and solve crimes. An example of such a database is the Automated Regional Justice Information System (ARJIS); it is a system that contains

> crime reports, arrest reports, field interview records, traffic citations, traffic accident reports, an alias file, and a variety of other kinds of records. It is used to identify suspects, clear suspects, track and identify trends and patterns of crime, and generate reports. . . . ARJIS is also used for crime analysis. It helps identify special crime problems and plan allocation of patrols. More than one million data entry and inquiry requests are processed by the system each month.[12]

Computers Provide Entertainment and Pleasure

Besides the economic, health, private, and public benefits that the computer revolution has made possible, computers have also affected the entertainment industry in a major way. Video games are becoming more complex, filmmakers have added new subtle and dramatic special effects, and the recording industry is learning to cope with music available online as new technology develops. The film industry can colorize old black-and-white movies or change the color of eyes with a few clicks of the computer mouse. These are developments that appeal to large audiences around the world.

The Computer Causes Intellectual-Property Problems

Along with the benefits, the computer revolution has also brought problems and risks, many which are still unsolved, and new problems arise as new technology becomes available. One problem has been the enforcement of intellectual-property rights. In the past, copyright laws protected authors and composers and assured their rights to control their works and receive compensation. Computer technology makes it easy to pirate creative works, thus denying the originators of those works just compensation. Schemes have been developed to persuade users to pay for downloading voluntarily, but none of the schemes has been successful. Currently developers are working on a CD that has a built-in mechanism to prevent its being downloaded. Moreover, the concept of intellectual property has expanded. Businesses have begun to include their trade secrets and marketing strategies in the category of intellectual property since the use of computer technology makes it harder to protect business ideas than it was when the information was on paper locked in files.

Computer Technology Raises Free-Speech Issues

Besides the problems relating to intellectual property, the free and open nature of the Internet also raises the issue of free speech and regulation, particularly in regard to pornography and the protection of children. Many states have laws against child pornography, but when technology is used to alter ordinary pictures to make them look pornographic, the issue becomes more complicated. In these instances, no real child has been subjected to pornography, but the difference between real and altered images is difficult to detect.

The issue of free speech and regulation also applies to adults. To protect free speech in a democratic society, the American Library Association has taken the position that all materials, including pornography, have to be available even when the source is the Internet in public libraries. Those who argue for free speech fear that regulation of the Internet is the first step that will ultimately threaten democracy and a free and open society. Those who argue for regulation claim that human rights are trampled when offensive material is imposed on people who do not want to be exposed to it. This problem emerged at the Minneapolis Public Library. Librarians complained that their rights were violated by the behavior of men who used library computers many hours at a time to view pornography. The librarians could not escape the pornography while doing their work, and because they needed their jobs, neither could they quit. Trying to solve this human rights problem is difficult and ongoing.

The Problem of Privacy

Health information stored on databases poses an issue of patient privacy. An insurance company with access to health care records could benefit financially by denying insurance to a patient with a chronic and costly disease; an employer may avoid hiring a worker with a high-risk health condition. The Department of Health and Human Services has recently issued final rules providing nationwide privacy protection. According to Lawrence O. Gostin, writing in the *Journal of the American Medical Association*,

> The rule is extensive in its scope, applying to health plans, health care clearinghouses, and health care providers (hospitals, clinics, and health departments) who conduct financial transactions electronically ("covered entities"). The rule applies to personally identifiable information in any form, whether communicated electronically, on paper, or orally. The rule does not preempt state law that affords more stringent privacy protection; thus, the health care industry will have to comply with multiple layers of federal and state law.[13]

According to the rule, patients have the right to education about privacy safeguards and access to their own medical records. The rule also includes a process for correcting errors in medical records and gives patients permission to have their records disclosed to designated persons. Clearly the need exists to protect the privacy of health care information from those who could abuse it, but there are legitimate reasons also to disclose such information. Epidemiologists need access to health care data to conduct research. Public Health Departments need access to records when an epidemic or community health problem arises. And sometimes, concerned relatives need information to help patients make health decisions. Health care rules need to be written in a way that protects patients but are flexible enough to permit disclosure when it is in the best interest of patients or the community.

An emerging technology using a new ultrasound system for tracking raises another kind of privacy issue. The system works like this: A person wears a small tracking device. It sends sound waves, which are picked up by receivers placed above the ceiling tiles throughout the building. The receivers measure the speed of the sound waves from the tracking device to the receivers and calculate the distance. The system then depicts a three-dimensional picture of the person wearing the device in the environment where he or she is located. This technology could quickly locate a doctor for an emergency. Although this technology could be very useful, it could also be misused, thus violating an individual's privacy.

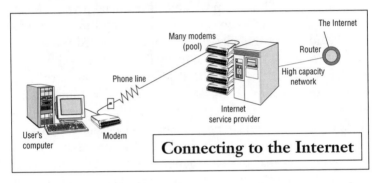

Connecting to the Internet

A device used to supervise workers is software that enables an employer to examine the keystrokes made on an office computer, a practice that is legal in many private corporations. On August 8, 2001, the *New York Times* featured a story about federal employees who disabled software that had been installed to check on them. If this software created enough anxiety for judicial workers to revolt, a device that tracks a worker's every move is likely to encounter at least as much resistance.

Protecting the privacy of financial information is harder than protecting health information because much of the financial information passes over the Internet. Companies can use e-commerce transactions to gather marketing information, and hackers can access the credit card numbers and bank records of other people. In 2000 the Senate proposed federal online privacy legislation, known as the Consumer

Internet Privacy Enhancement Act. Writing in *Precision Marketing*, Clive Walker explains, "Sponsored by US senators John McCain, John Kerry, Spencer Abraham and Barbara Boxer, the Bill orders E-commerce sights to be 'clear and conspicuous' about how and why data is collected. Consumers must also have the option to stop their data being used for marketing purposes."[14] Large Internet companies, in particular the Walt Disney Internet Group with its 23 million visitors a month, favor this legislation because it provides consistent rules all across the United States. The Federal Trade Commission and state attorneys general have the power to enforce disclosure requirements. This legislation does not solve all of the problems of financial privacy, but it provides the power to enforce laws involving Internet crime.

The advent of the wireless Internet has caused greater security problems. Even though many IT (Internet technology) departments have hesitated to deploy wireless infrastructure, companies making handsets are already manufacturing phones ready for the Internet, pushing IT departments toward building a wireless infrastructure. The security danger is real. In one country, hackers broke into a system and forced cell phones to dial the emergency number. The volume of calls shut down the emergency network. Hackers in another country sent a disparaging message over the network of the country's large telecommunications provider. Although this event lacked the same life-or-death nature of the emergency network break-in, it did reveal that the wireless networks are vulnerable. The security flaws in wireless also mean that hackers can enter the system and obtain information while a person makes a financial transaction or transfers valuable information, exposing the network to potential theft. Nonetheless, companies look forward to the day when security problems are solved and they can deploy wireless technology.

Faster, More Powerful Computers in the Future

Computer experts say that the number of transistors that can be placed on a computer chip is limited, and chips are reaching the limits. Consequently, scientists are searching for alternatives—new kinds of circuits that will run computers faster and give them greater power. One current project is quantum computing. With this scheme, a computer uses radio waves to manipulate atoms that in turn power the computer. This method has the advantage of being able to do two calculations at once, according to the laws of quantum mechanics. George Johnson, writing for the *New York Times* says, "The goal, still but a distant glimmer, is to harness thousands of atoms, resulting in a machine so powerful that it would easily break codes now considered impenetrable and solve other problems that are impossible for even the fastest supercomputer."[15]

Another team of scientists at Lucent Technologies' Bell Labs is working on the use of DNA strands to make circuits. In "DNA Molecules May Nanofabricate Future Computers," Pieter Burggraaf explains the effort "to attach DNA to electrically conducting molecules to assemble rudimentary molecular-scale electric circuits. The eventual application may result in computers that are 100x more powerful than today's systems."[16] These experiments in technology could provide new kinds of circuits with more speed and power to replace the present transistors that are reaching their limits.

Ideas for New Computer Projects

Some of the ideas and plans for new technology are small and frivolous, and others extend over vast time and space. One example enhances the skill of a local fisherman. Speculating from a contour map of a favorite fishing lake, Ray Sasser of the *Dallas Morning News* imagines a computer cartographer devising a three-dimensional view of the lake bottom. He speculates further:

> How about a computer program where you highlight a favorite fishing hole and ask the computer to show you similar spots?

> I can easily envision a techno-angler with a battery-powered laptop cruising the lake and learning more about its hidden secrets in a day or two than serious weekend fishermen have discovered through trial and error in the lake's 20-year history.[17]

Another example enhances the commercialization of space. A joint government and industry group is working on

InterPlaNetary (IPN) Internet, a system to be developed in stages for communication among spaceships, robots, and manned and unmanned outposts in the solar system. It will work as a network of Internets, which will carry information from a gateway on Earth to a gateway on Mars, for example, in a "new, end-to-end 'bundle' protocol."[18] This project is the stuff of minds that envision mining projects on asteroids, hotels in space, and zero-gravity manufacturing and medicine.

Imaginative Projects Still in the Laboratories

Engineers in corporate laboratories around the globe have developed new technologies that are still several years from the retail level. For example, Holger Regenbrecht, an engineer for a major car company, has designed augmented reality (AR) glasses. With them he can see two levels of images: the real car engine and also an animated three-dimensional digital image superimposed on the real image. Gregory Beals, in "The Future of Computers," describes how the glasses work: "He sees the air-intake nozzle he needs to replace outlined in bright red. He follows the animated arrows right in front of his eyes. Usually one of the more complicated parts of an engine to replace, the nozzle slides into place without a hitch."[19]

This accomplishment means that the computer has to "see" and comprehend what it is looking at. A tiny digicam, fitted to the side of the glasses, tracks the wearer's field of vision, and software then fits the virtual engine to the real engine and shows the images on the glasses. Though the glasses have a cumbersome design now, future glasses will have a streamlined look suitable for other purposes. Beals explains several possible uses:

> AR glasses that would allow a surgeon to "see" a patient's CT scan as he operates. In Greece a tourist-information system based on AR is being planned for the 2006 Olympics; visitors will receive wearable PCs and funky goggles that will let them amble through digital re-creations of the ancient ruins of Olympia. And a Japanese firm is building an AR computer game with virtual monsters.[20]

Engineers in other laboratories are designing new ways of making computer screens. One is as thin as a sheet of paper. On this Internet paper, the text will change to display the next page when the reader's eyes get to the bottom of the page. Another, by a Japanese researcher named Jun Rekimoto, expands digital technology to make ordinary walls and tables function as display screens that can be used interactively. This technology incorporates cameras, palm-size devices, laptops, and mobile phones all wired to the Internet. If a dress designer, for example, sitting in a conference preparing for a fashion show sees a flaw in a dress, she can use her mouse to drag an image of the dress to the table top, use her special pen to change the dimension of it, and send the change to the dressmaker in another location. Rekimoto "believes that the future of computing lies not in loading up old objects with gadgetry but in creating a digital work space in which ordinary objects can interface for new computers."[21]

A Japanese robotics engineer, Yoshihiro Fujita, is working on the R-100 personal-computer robot, a cross between a robot and a PC, whose specialty is computer vision. He wants the R-100 to be a true helper, even when its owner is away; it could find the availability of seats for performances, access e-mail when told to, and guard the house. R-100 is equipped with a Pentium-based computer-processing unit, two cameras, and high-sensitivity microphones. Fujita believes that future robots will play an important social role: "Elderly people may someday use a robot like R-100 to write letters or download information on medicines from the doctor's office. The infirm might rely on a robot to remind them to take their medicine. 'The robot will be a useful post-PC device,' he says. Perhaps it will even become man's best friend."[22]

A final example of the projects that researchers are working on in their laboratories is a perceptual interface, a computer that understands language and has enough common sense to grasp the speaker's intentions without having every detail spelled out. Japanese researcher Yoichi Takebayashi cites the example of driving toward Mount Fuji. The driver asks the dashboard computer how far away the mountain is, and the computer responds verbally that it is twenty miles away. The driver then asks for a list of hiking trails. The computer selects the list appropriate for the driver because it already knows that the driver likes bird watching and because it already knows the driver has had a recent knee injury and needs easy trails. This computer is wired with speakers, microphones, displays, software that can pick out key words in a sentence and give them meaning, and, most importantly, software agents. Agents are computer programs with several functions: They complete the requests made to them, such as finding the map; they retain a history of how the driver used the agents in the past; and they store a record of the driver's preferences. "Your agent would know about your bum knee because it probably scheduled the initial doctor's visit. To marry these two difficult technologies is clearly a long-term challenge. It will be a long time before we can talk to computers the way we do to each other."[23]

A New Beginning or Fast-Forwarded Tendencies?

The research of recent days, which experiments with wireless technology and several technologies bundled together to accomplish complicated tasks, suggests that the post-PC era has arrived. The new products will undoubtedly change the way people live and work in profound ways. In 1981 Howard Rosenbrock thought that the computer revolution would not be a new beginning nor would it uproot life as the Industrial Revolution had done in England, but instead the computer revolution would make dramatic changes by intensifying and extending old tendencies. Twenty years later, he seems both right and wrong. He is right that mass populations of people have not been uprooted to settle in new locations. Most people today still go to work in the schools, businesses, factories, and hospitals where they have been working for years. Rosenbrock is definitely right in his prediction that life would move faster and become more intense than before. But he seems to have missed the psychological effects that the computers are having on society. They are uprooting traditional thinking about communities and the world, traditional attitudes toward machines, and traditional assumptions about how people use and control machines.

Today's computer technology makes the globe seem smaller and creates expectations that things happen faster, but it leaves individuals less assured of whether they are in control of the machine, enamored of it, or controlled by it. The moderator of the *Discover*-Disney panel asked the panelists,

> Are we on the cusp of a different moment in our evolution as a species, where our intersection and interaction with a tool become something that is deeper and more profound than it has been before?

> Story Musgrave [answered]: I think you really strike on something there when you talk about emotional relationships with inanimate objects.[24]

The final conclusion of whether the computer revolution is a new beginning or an extension and intensification of old tendencies is a question best left for future historians.

Notes

1. Quoted in *Discover*, "The Startling Future of Computers," November 1999, p. 63.

2. Sara Baase, *A Gift of Fire: Social, Legal, and Ethical Issues in Computing*. Upper Saddle River, NJ: Prentice Hall, 1997, p. 2.

3. Quoted in Tom Forester, ed., *The Information Technology Revolution*. Cambridge, MA: MIT Press, 1985, pp. 641–42.

4. *Economist*, "The Age of the Cloud: A Survey of Software," April 14, 2001, p. 3.

5. Quoted in Baase, *A Gift of Fire*, p. 7.

6. Quoted in Forester, *The Information Technology Revolution*, p. 285.

7. David O. Arnold, *Computers and Society: Impact!* New York: McGraw-Hill, 1991, pp. 270–71.

8. Bill Gates, with Collins Hemingway, *Business @ the Speed of Thought: Using a Digital Nervous System*. New York: Warner Books, 1999, p. 134.

9. Christopher T. Heun, "Virtual Exams Hit the Road," *Information Week*, March 26, 2001, p. 20.

10. *American Medical News*, "Doctors Say Computers Have Positive Impact, Survey Finds," April 9, 2001, p. 28.

11. Baase, *A Gift of Fire*, p. 18.

12. Baase, *A Gift of Fire*, pp. 19–20.

13. Lawrence O. Gostin, "National Health Information Privacy: Regulations Under the Health Insurance Portability and Accounting Act," *Journal of the American Medical Association*, June 20, 2001, p. 3,015.

14. Clive Walker, "Disney Backs US Web Legislation," *Precision Marketing*, October 16, 2000, p. 10.

15. George Johnson, "Computing One Atom at a Time," *New York Times*, March 27, 2001, Midwest edition.

16. Pieter Burggraaf, "DNA Molecules May Nanofabricate Future," *Solid State Technology*, October 2000, p. 30.

17. Ray Sasser, "Wave of Future: Laptop Computers for Techno-Anglers," *Dallas Morning News*, June 21, 2000.

18. Gary H. Anthes, "Internet to Mars," *Computerworld*, July 16, 2001, p. 50.

19. Gregory Beals, "The Future of Computers," *Newsweek International*, June 18, 2001, p. 44.

20. Quoted in Beals, "The Future of Computers," p. 44.

21. Beals, "The Future of Computers," p. 44.

22. Beals, "The Future of Computers," p. 44.

23. Beals, "The Future of Computers," p. 44.

24. *Discover,* "The Startling Future of Computers," p. 63.

Chapter 1

The History and Identification of Computer Technology

History of the Computer

Gene I. Rochlin

Gene I. Rochlin explains the development of the computer industry, beginning with the U.S. government support of computer research after World War II. In the first stage, before the invention of the transistor, computers were huge, centrally located, and unreliable. In the second stage, according to Rochlin, progress in the semiconductor industry made possible the design of computers small enough for installation in research laboratories and universities. The third stage saw the emergence of personal computers and the standardized programs of Microsoft's DOS and Windows. Rochlin, professor of energy and resources at the University of California at Berkeley, received a John D. and Catherine T. MacArthur Foundation fellowship for his research and writing in international security.

The history of computer hardware is in itself fascinating, and important. Without the incredible pace of hardware development, miniaturization, and decreased cost that followed the introduction of solid-state electronics, there would have been no computer revolution, and the social and political effects on which this book focuses would never have been possible. But hardware in itself cannot be an agent for change. In the case of the computer, coevolution with software made the difference; despite market-driven races to develop faster and ever more powerful hardware, and despite fierce and often nasty competition between suppliers of software to capture market share through specific features, it is the nature of the application, not the machine, or the programming, that attracts potential users.

U.S. Government Supports Computer Research

As with nuclear energy and a number of other fields that had once been the subject primarily of scientific inquiry and discourse, the development of the electronic digital computer was greatly spurred by the Second World War. Although the purposes were at first narrow and specialized, the concentration of the research community and the comparatively huge resources given to it were to form the foundation of the postwar effort, with continuing governmental support. The government also continued to support the initial development of programming languages and other fundamental software that became central in remaking computers into general-purpose analytical tools, electronic successors to [British inventor] Charles Babbage's dream of a generalized "difference engine." Over time, the capabilities were transferred for use by developers and government agencies, and then for large, central firms doing considerable government business.

Those who got their start in one or another of the early military projects, or consulted for them, eventually moved out into private industry in search of uses, applications, and markets. But the military roots remained, and it was not until the 1960s that commercial markets grew large enough to support a fully independent industry. As the computer revolution picked up speed, entrepreneurs and just plain technical enthusiasts moved in, and most of the hardware and software now in common use was developed specifically for commercial applications. Much of what remains of direct government support is focused on the formulation of specific equipment and specific software for dedicated purposes.

But the U.S. government continues to see the development of advanced computer techniques as having important implications for national security (i.e., military) purposes, and therefore remains heavily invested in supporting fundamental, forefront research, particularly in high status areas such as artificial intelligence. This also has consequences. The community of government-supported superstars, often far removed from real users or immediate needs, continues to shape the attitudes of programmers throughout the entire industry both by example and by its ability to shape the goals and beliefs of the social universe in which designers live and work. And that universe in turn was formed and shaped by the history of the industry.

The Development of Huge Mainframe Computers

The first large, digital computers were hardly more than electric realizations of Charles Babbage's difference engine (and many were barely electronic). Their purpose was primarily to perform huge calculations rapidly and accurately (i.e., what they computed were numerical results, such as firing tables for large artillery and naval guns), and the operation of each was done through a tedious and usually quite idiosyncratic process of setting up a calculational program through the setting of an enormous number of switches and patches. In those early days, progress was measured largely by increases in the size and capacity of the machines. As it was widely believed that the total social demand for computers at this scale was for no more than a few dozen, or a few hundred, machines—large, expensive, and run by in-house experts—there was no particular reason or economic motive for the development of general, nonproprietary software or simplified front ends for operation.

The invention of the transistor and the creation of the integrated circuit caused a major reorganization and redesign of the nascent industry. Smaller, faster, more reliable, and with much simpler requirements for power and cooling than their vacuum-tube predecessors, machines using solid-state circuitry revolutionized every aspect of electronics from simple radios to the most complicated computers. In only a few years, the huge, ungainly machines that gave off enormous quantities of heat, and whose time of continuous operation between failures might be measured in hours, or at best days, were completely superseded by solid-state, integrated-circuit machines that were inherently faster and far more reliable. The failure rate of the first solid-state computers was orders of magnitude smaller than that of their vacuum-tube predecessors.

Because of their size, cost, and complexity, the commercial manufacture of the first mainframe computers was a task not to be entered into lightly. The field soon came to be dominated by a few large firms, including a preexisting corporate giant—IBM—that gained knowledge from government contracts and access through the reputation and experience it had gained from dominating the market of electromechanical office equipment. IBM controlled half the market by 1955, only two years after its entry, and more than 65 percent by 1965, when the business had become known as "IBM and the Seven Dwarfs." Although other companies continued to compete, it was IBM that determined the course of development.

The situation as of the mid-1960s has been neatly summarized by [computer specialist] Larry Roberts:

> In 1964 only large mainframe computers existed, each with its own separate set of users. If you were lucky the computer was time-shared, but even then you could not go far away since the terminals were hard-wired to it or connected by local phone line. Moreover, if you wanted data from another computer, you moved it by tape and you could forget wanting software from a different type of computer.

Such standards as existed for moving data about were mostly set by IBM, which had adopted its familiar accounting technology, the Hollerith[1] punched card (modeled in turn on the cards used for more than a century to program Jacquard[2] looms), as a method for providing input. Even the later development of magnetic storage and standardized programming did not free users from being tied by their computers and terminals to a set of very restricted environments.

Technical and systems evolution had gone down the same socio-historical path as the classic infrastructure technologies of the early part of the century, with one important exception. Although expansion and growth were still controlled by managers who judged them by actual performance and real returns, the large, centralized, computer centers that emerged,

1. Herman Hollerith received a patent in 1889 for a machine using punch cards in census taking. 2. Joseph-Marie Jacquard created a system of punch cards to keep track of patterns on nineteenth-century looms.

and still dominate many companies and government organizations, seemed forbidding, remote, and, with their cadre of experts speaking arcane languages, sometimes threatening. The combination of the isolation of the centers with the presumed power of computers they operated became a focal point for a public that increasingly felt that technical change was threatening loss of control in "modern" societies. As such, they became the obvious target of manifestations of social concern about the future, in forums ranging from editorials to popular art. What few people realized was that the mainframes were dinosaurs, soon to be almost completely displaced except for specialized purposes such as running huge, complex mathematical models.

Designers Use Semiconductors to Create a Small Computer

What did survive, however, was a rather unique social-organizational legacy, the creation and empowerment of a small cadre of hardware and software designers and highly trained operators whose special skills and special languages isolated them from the rest of the organization and left them free to pursue their own design and developmental goals. Given the cost of the new computer centers, and the need to justify both their existence and their budgets, these internal desires were always subject to rather strict limitations. But the precedent of autonomy and control had been set.

Progress in the semiconductor industry, driven in part by the search for defense-related applications, proceeded at a ferocious pace that has not yet let up; every year, components continue to get smaller, cheaper, faster, and more complex. During the 1960s, solid-state circuitry had progressed sufficiently to significantly lower the costs of entry into the burgeoning computer market, triggering a second developmental wave that was to carry the computer industry far from its megalithic beginnings in less than a decade. Although IBM continued to exploit the decreasing size and cost of solid-state circuitry to improve and expand mainframes, a new entrepreneurial firm, Digital Equipment Corporation (DEC), chose to avoid competing with IBM by producing a line of "mini" computers—small but powerful laboratory and business machines that did not require specially prepared and conditioned rooms. Eventually, the minicomputers were to become small enough to actually be placed next to a desk, or even on top of one. More to the point, they were to expand the community of programmers to include a large number of people independent of both hardware manufacturers and large, centralized computer operations.

Because the DEC machines were particularly flexible and powerful, and because DEC welcomed participation and involvement from the research community, their machines quickly became popular in laboratories and universities. With the introduction of UNIX™, an adaptable and open operating system that had been developed by AT&T's Bell Laboratories and widely disseminated for a nominal fee, DEC/UNIX systems and networks became ubiquitous in research laboratories, universities, and, eventually, classrooms across the country.

Mainframes were fine for grinding out big, difficult calculations; as a means for communication, the new art of text processing, or performing simpler tasks, they were at best clumsy. The relative openness and transparency of the UNIX system, the power and simplicity of the high-order programming language (C) that had also been developed at Bell Laboratories and in which it was coded, and the incredible facilitation of interpersonal networking, at first at individual sites and then among them, created expectations and demands in the community of sophisticated users that could not be easily fulfilled by centrally controlled hierarchical computer centers and large, powerful mainframes. . . .

While researchers back East were concentrating on the minicomputer transformation, an eclectic collection of electronic tinkerers were working in garages and workshops around the San Francisco Bay Area on something even smaller. Many had dropped out of major computer corporations to pursue the dream of a computer that was entirely one's own, often overlaid with a libertarian philosophy that blended the radical and communitarian thought that emerged during the upheavals of the 1960s with the traditional Ameri-

Babbage's Computing Machines

In The Social Impact of Computers, *Richard S. Rosenberg describes the computing machines of British mathematician and inventor Charles Babbage. Called the father of the computer, Babbage began building a "difference engine" in 1821 and an "analytical engine" in 1836. He had neither the resources nor the skill to complete either machine.*

It was not until the mid–nineteenth century that a generally successful calculator became available. Charles Babbage (1792–1871), a most remarkable man—mathematician, inventor, and initiator of scientific management—flourished in this period. Undoubtedly, he deserves the title father of the computer. Ironically, his story is one of generally unfulfilled ambition. In 1821, he became interested in building a "Difference Engine" to automate the calculation of algebraic functions by using successive differences. A story describes the moment of its inception. Apparently Babbage was checking some calculations with John Herschel (the son of Sir William Herschel, the discoverer of Uranus) when Babbage remarked, "I wish to God these calculations had been executed by steam." Herschel simply replied, "It is quite possible." (Steam was the major power source of Babbage's time.)

can dream of the independent small business entrepreneur. Of necessity, the resulting machine would have to be relatively small, simple, and inexpensive; easy to maintain and upgrade; and convenient to program and operate.

In 1971, a small Silicon Valley company called Intel announced the result of two years of research—an integrated circuit that put the essentials of a computer on a single chip. Christened the *microprocessor,* the Intel chip was fully programmable despite its small size. The microchips seemed destined to the arcane world of pocket calculators until, in 1974, [electronics designer] Ed Roberts decided to build a computer kit. When the Altair hit the market in 1975, the response was almost frenzied. The following year, 1976, was the *annus mirabilis*[3] of the microcomputer transformation.

3. "wonderful year"; a period of extraordinary significance or production

In 1836, before his Difference Engine was completed, Babbage conceived of a much more powerful, general purpose computer that he called the Analytical Engine. In the end, neither machine was completed, for a variety of reasons—lack of sufficient financial resources, technical requirements beyond the skill available, and a design that underwent too-frequent change. There is little doubt, however, that Babbage at this early date envisioned a machine of such scope that its power would not be realized for more than a hundred years. His design included a memory store, an arithmetic unit, punched card input and output, and a mechanism that provided enough power of control to do iteration and branching. Following his death, others tried to build similar machines with little success. When successful machines were finally built, some of their designers were aware of his work; others were not. In the final analysis, Babbage appears to have been a cranky genius with ideas impossible to realize—for both economical and technical reasons—in his time.

Richard S. Rosenberg, *The Social Impact of Computers*. San Diego: Academic Press, 1992.

From Silicon Valley and its surroundings flowed the commercial realizations of the intelligent video display terminal and the miniaturized floppy disk, the first standardized bus, BASIC, CP/M, the first programming languages for microcomputers, Electric Pencil, the first microcomputer word processor. And linking them all together was the Homebrew computer club, the irreverent, anarchic, thinktank of the new industry.

Development of the PC

The third wave of computing emerged from what was quite literally a garage operation in California, when Steve Wozniak designed the Apple I, primarily to impress the club. The Apple I was hardly more than a circuit board, but its successor, the landmark Apple II of 1977, was the prototype of every desktop machine. Using a keyboard for input instead of toggle switches, with a video display system instead of blinking lights, and with a small, flexible (floppy) magnetic disk for storage, it is as recognizable to the modern user as a Model T—to which it might be aptly compared, for the widespread adoption of the Apple II and the word spread by its dedicated users reconstructed the meaning and image of electronic digital computing.

Given that DEC and others had already appropriated the term minicomputer for their now midsized models, the Apple and its descendants came to be referred to by the somewhat inappropriate appellation of *microcomputers*, perhaps because of the microprocessors that lay at their heart. The most familiar term in use today, however, is the one that IBM appropriated in 1981 for its first ever desktop computer—the *personal* computer, or PC. At first, the person in question was far more likely to be a computer professional or dedicated hobbyist than a typical office worker or member of the general public. The hardware was nice enough, but what was it for?

Standardizing Operating Systems

In the world of mainframes and minicomputers, the proprietary nature of operating systems was to some degree compensated for by islands of standardization in programming software, some promoted by the government and some by business and corporate interests. Having been deliberately developed outside of those worlds, software and operating systems for the first personal computers were even more chaotic and idiosyncratic than the machines themselves. At one time, for example, almost every manufacturer, including those who had standardized on the same Intel chip and the same underlying operating system, used a unique format for floppy disks. Exchange of software and data between users was a trying and often frustrating experience—when it could be done at all.

As with the historical cases of automobiles, electricity, and telephones, increasing acceptance and use was accompanied by a demand for standardization. Over time, two primary standards emerged—that of Apple computer, closely tied to and integrated with its own hardware, and the more open system that serves not only the descendants of the first IBM PC, but the world of clones that now dominate the microcomputer market. . . .

The rest, as they say, is history. The standardized, reliable PC with its new operating system, carrying the respected logo of IBM, was welcomed into homes and offices with an eagerness that no one in the industry could ever have imagined. Within only a year, the term "PC" had entered the common language as the generic term for a desktop microcomputer. Sales soared, and by 1983, *Time* magazine had a computer on its cover as the "machine of the year." Within a few years, PC systems with MS-DOS and standardized disk formats and software had created a whole new market, pushing CP/M and other competing systems aside. Small, entrepreneurial companies either adapted or found their market share shriveling to a narrow and specialized niche.

Over time, the story acquires an ironic twist. As the PC market expanded, IBM failed to keep up with the cutting edge, either in perceived performance or in price. The open architecture of the PC and the easy license requirements of DOS made possible the rapid worldwide spread of PC "clones" that reduced not only IBM's share of the market but its position as market leader and standard bearer. What did become standard was Microsoft's DOS, in all of its variants, and, later, not only its own line of specialized programs, but a visual interface, Microsoft's Windows™, that replicated in purpose, if not precisely in detail, the mice-and-menus approach of the Macintosh.

In 1981, when you said PC, you meant IBM. By the 1990s, the future development of PCs was largely in the hands of Intel, maker of the continually evolving line of processor chips that lay at the heart of the machine, and Microsoft, maker of operating systems and software.

The Computer Revolution Raises New Questions

M. David Ermann, Mary B. Williams,
and Claudio Gutierrez

M. David Ermann, Mary B. Williams, and Claudio Gutierrez survey new issues evolving with the computer revolution. Regarding business ethics, the authors ask if workers'
rights will be protected when companies can gather volumes of personal information without consent and monitor their employees' activities. They address the advantages and disadvantages of the home as a workplace and of
the completely automated workplace. On the global scale,
the authors ponder the possibility that millions of workers
will be displaced by computers. All three authors are fac-
ulty members at the University of Delaware. Ermann, who
teaches sociology, is the coauthor of *Corporate Deviance*;
Williams teaches philosophy; and Gutierrez is a computer
science professor.

Like any powerful tool, computers can be a force for good
or harm. They can give physicians instant access to all of the
information available on a patient in crisis, but they can also
give unscrupulous charlatans the names of all cancer patients. They can give a business important new control over
its inventory, but they can also give it privacy-invading control over its employees. Computerized robots might make
work obsolete while producing abundance for everyone, but
they can also throw millions of people into unemployment
and poverty. To maximize the benefits and minimize the
harms, those making decisions about the implementation of
computer systems (e.g., programmers, systems designers,

computer scientists, managers, legislators) must be sensitive to the potential problems as well as to the potential advantages of computers.

Because the computer gives us fundamentally new power, we are faced with decisions for which our experiences may give little guidance. The danger of applying old standards to a fundamentally new situation is well illustrated by the law, passed soon after the production of the first automobiles, which required cars traveling the roads to be preceded by a man on foot carrying a red flag. This law reduced danger, but robbed the auto of its intrinsic power. Similarly we could stop one type of computer crime by outlawing electronic fund transfer, or prevent a potentially dangerous accumulation of governmental power by outlawing the interconnection of computers storing different sets of information about individuals, or prevent robots from taking workers' jobs by outlawing robotization. It is possible to respond to every danger by cutting off the power that leads to that danger. But it is more productive to respond by analyzing each situation as it occurs. This way, we may conclude that our fundamental values are better served by changing our expectations or rules rather than by denying ourselves opportunities to take advantage of what the computer can do. Such an analysis requires some understanding both of the social problems that computers may cause and of the nature of our moral system. . . .

Computers can be used in many ways by business: to automate work processes, to monitor employees' work and efficiency, to maintain massive amounts of personnel data, and even to reduce building and transportation costs by having employees work at home using the telecommunication features of computers. Each of these uses has potential risks and benefits.

Balancing Monitoring of Employees with Workers' Rights

Thanks to computers, for instance, managers now can monitor employees' business calls, their minute-by-minute work patterns, and the time they spend in contact with customers.

Already [at the beginning of the 1990s], about 5 million workers, mostly in clerical or repetitive jobs, have some or all of their work evaluated on the basis of computer-generated data, and many more have computer-generated data collected but not currently used in evaluation. This information, according to critics, can invade employees' privacy, reduce their personal dignity, and even affect their health. Consider the case of Patricia Johnson, a post office employee in Washington, D.C. She sorts fifty letters per minute, remembering thousands of addresses in two zip codes in order to assign each letter correctly to one of seventy letter carriers. And now computerization allows her supervisor to watch her like a hawk, creating greater stress than she previously experienced: "The mail is running by me and running by me and the machine kind of hypnotizes you. And this computer is looking over your shoulder, watching you. It gets very stressful. . . . The supervisor knows everything about you, right in that machine."

Of course, Patricia Johnson's experience may reflect our current inability to use computers to full advantage. In the future, computers may become less tools for external supervision and more integrated aids to workers. For instance, computers may revolutionize the conditions of office work. Technologists are already experimenting on artificial intelligence–inspired systems that actually create a worker/machine partnership and coordinate the interactions of different workstations. These integrated systems keep track of relationships among administrative tasks and subtasks, of peoples' promises to complete tasks, and of actual fulfillment of tasks. The result is an environment in which the worker has up-to-date information about which of his unfinished tasks is most crucial to the system. Such a partnership between worker and computer might well increase the worker's job satisfaction and decrease the need for external supervision.

Large organizations are ravenous information consumers. Because computers can collect, process, and exchange massive quantities of information, they can help corporations violate an individual's rights. The potential for misuse of some information about employees is inescapable. Many employers have tried to counter the possibility of misuse of personnel records by initiating policies that limit the amount of computerized (and other) data in employee records. Control Data Corporation's policy, for instance, states that individually identifiable employee records should be collected only if justified by the needs of (1) a specific business decision, (2) payroll, benefits, or other administrative procedures, or (3) requirements of government reporting. The policy addresses four ways employee records could be used unfairly: asking for unneeded information; gathering information in unfair ways (e.g., polygraphs, secret investigations); failing to keep accurate and complete records; and failing to properly restrict access to records. Among policies adopted to regulate data collection are requirements that employees be informed of data acquired "through interfaces with external organizations (insurance carriers, credit card companies, etc.)," and that the company not collect or store information regarding "political opinions, religious or other beliefs and sex life" of employees [as is the policy of] Control Data Corporation, 1984. Doubters point out that such prohibitions are nice, but they are not always obeyed.

Advantages and Disadvantages of Working at Home

The introduction of computers for work in the home, as a total or partial substitute for work at the office or factory, creates additional concerns. On the one hand, there are specialized professionals, like computer programmers, for whom work at home has many advantages and few disadvantages. Conversely, there are the legions of office workers for whom working at home will result in lower salaries and benefits. Unions systematically oppose such arrangements, both because the dispersion of workers is inimical to the esprit de corps so important for mobilizing members to fight for better conditions, and because the history of home-work arrangements is replete with worker exploitation. (Such fears might cause a union to oppose a proffered arrangement that is actually beneficial to the workers.) Additional disadvantages for at-home workers are less visibility for promotion, problems with supervision and security of sensitive materials, and diminished interaction among co-workers. But there are also advantages: more availability of jobs for parents with small children, for the handicapped, and for the aged; better integration between personal and work life; more and better time for recreation (avoidance of weekend crowds); and savings on fuel and clothes.

Computerization Within the Workplace

Finally, consider the worker experience with wholesale computerization within a workplace. Computers can be responsible for deskilling workers; for fragmenting complex jobs into small, meaningless pieces, each done by a different person; for reducing the skill and initiative and hence the psychic rewards of a job; and for making work machine-paced and hence out of the control of workers. Past technologies, particularly the assembly line, have done this. Computers can also reduce the total number of jobs available. Virtually all studies suggest that computers eliminate more jobs than they create, though (predictably) studies sponsored by unions and liberal groups show greater reductions than studies sponsored by managements and conservative groups.

We would suggest that the pessimists are correct on the reduction of total employment, while the optimists are correct about the nature of work. Computers have eliminated more jobs than they have created, and will continue to do so. But, with important exceptions such as the use of computer controls for machine tools, they have not deskilled many jobs. Deskilling has already been accomplished by the assembly line and other methods of speeding production; the computer is putting important skills, responsibilities, and autonomy back into jobs. This was clearly illustrated by past research, and by interviews our students conducted with people who recently had computers introduced into their work. Secretaries overwhelmingly liked the improved quality and quantity of work they produced, and the fact that they knew more about the computer than their bosses did. Factory workers being retrained at a newly computerized automobile plant said that in the past they were hired from their neck down, but now they could use their heads as well. The computerization of the plant caused great anxiety and the loss of 1,300 jobs (held by those with the least social power and the fewest skills). But it is hard to imagine how the computer could have further deskilled the jobs of auto assemblers, and it seems instead to have enhanced skills used in this type of work.

Experiences with Computers

From 1986 to 1989, each of our students interviewed two people who experienced significant computerization in a work setting that previously had not been computerized. Based on the 200-plus interview reports submitted, our students' research suggested that people tended to approve of computerization of their workplaces when

1. their jobs were not threatened by the computer. White-collar workers were least likely to feel that computers might cause them to lose their jobs.
2. their skills and responsibilities were upgraded, or they received supervisory approval for their new skills and outputs. Though the computer tended to enhance skills in both blue-collar and white-collar settings, it was particularly job-enhancing in office work. People with office jobs also appreciated the feeling of being at the cutting edge of their occupations.
3. their job productivity increased, or their tedious and unvalued job routines or clerical work declined. This satisfaction increase was greatest for people who placed relatively more emphasis on efficiency than on inter-personal relations.
4. their personal control over their work increased. Those in assembly work and typing pools tended not to get this increased control.
5. they were young, or they were older and felt proud of overcoming their initial anxieties.

Computers also had negative side effects for a minority of our interviewees. Some respondents reported that:
1. interpersonal contact declined, as accountants, travel

agents, supervisors, analysts, and others had fewer reasons to consult in person with colleagues at nearby desks or down the hall.

2. privacy declined, as others could monitor employees' work, send junk-mail messages, and in one case access private information.
3. tension increased when the computers they had learned to depend on were down for more than a few seconds.

Our conclusion is that computers tend to give the greatest rewards to young, white-collar, technologically comfortable, and organizationally secure people who can use computers to gain increased satisfaction from their work.

Computerization of a factory appears to bring with it a pattern of improved working conditions—for those who are not laid off—as illustrated in the General Motors assembly plant near our university in Delaware, and the General Electric Appliance Park in Louisville, Kentucky. In both cases, employment dropped drastically. At G.E., it dropped from 19,000 to 10,000 in one decade. On the positive side, however, jobs of the remaining workers were less narrowly prescribed, leaving more room for individual initiative; and the company made concerted and somewhat successful efforts to improve the skills of workers, to listen to their suggestions, and to give them more control of the pace of the assembly line and the ability to stop it when problems arise. In sum, in the United States and other economically developed societies, computers cost more jobs than they create, but improve many of the jobs that remain.

Advanced Communication on the International Level

On an international level, advances in communications through the use of cable, telephone lines, or satellite links make possible the transmission of data across national boundaries. But even though we might expect that the mobility of information would accelerate technical progress all over the world, facilitate world commerce, and help to solve the special needs of underdeveloped countries, in fact it seems that this is not happening. There are good reasons to believe that computers help the dominant classes of third-world nations form alliances with their counterparts in industrialized countries, while at the same time putting distance between themselves and the impoverished majorities in their own countries. The new technology thus seems to be increasing rather than decreasing the gap between rich and poor in the third world. The basic reasons for this are that advanced technology requires high levels of education which the underprivileged of the world lack, and that the desired goods of the information age are "knowledge-intensive" rather than "labor-intensive." Since the underprivileged have only their labor to sell, their position seems likely to become worse as computerization increases.

Reactions to these worrisome facts are varied. Some think this is only a temporary phenomenon which will soon be overcome by global transformations of a more positive character. They mention the precedent of the industrial revolution, when prophecies of doom about explosive unemployment did not come true because the very energy of the revolution created new and better jobs for displaced workers. But, as [computer expert Nils J.] Nilsson points out in his essay "Artificial Intelligence, Employment, and Income," there is something new and eminently different about the information revolution. The displaced labor force of the industrial revolution retreated from dangerous jobs, or jobs that required great physical effort, or were repetitive and unintellectual; most of these people then found more interesting and intellectually satisfying jobs in the area of services and state or private bureaucracies. But the new technological unemployment is eliminating the types of jobs that the industrial revolution brought into being. With the exception of the robotization of industry, computerization is occurring and will continue to occur mainly in areas (like banking, commerce, and administration) where displaced workers do not have the alternatives that their predecessors had during the industrial revolution.

For the first time in history, therefore, many of the unemployed may not be able to find a new job, interesting or otherwise. It is clear that this qualitatively new problem has to be faced in ways which will be profoundly distinct and for which there is little precedent. With the elimination of work opportunities by the progressive automation of the intellectual functions in factories, stores, and offices, large masses of the population will lose their means of support. If they join the present unemployed as marginal citizens, they will become a sign of our moral failure to create a humane computerized world.

The question then becomes how to provide incomes to people when there is not enough work to go around. Is it sufficient to keep diminishing the weekly hours of work, to use early retirement, and to protract the years of formal education? Louis Kelso and Mortimer Adler anticipated this situation and proposed drastic measures of economic reform in the *Capitalist Manifesto*. These authors explored the possibility of having a society of "owners," in which every citizen receives his/her income from ownership of machines (intelligent robots) that produce all the necessary goods of society without the need for human labor (apart from governance and the administration of property). In such a society, people would end up occupying positions similar to the owners of slaves; being owner of the means of production, they would avoid servile toil and concentrate on governance and administration, the practice of the sciences and the arts, the cultivation of friendship, sports, and the like.

But how can we make a transition to such a utopia? History teaches us that the powerful are unlikely to altruistically relinquish much of their economic power in order to benefit the weak. The industrial revolution resulted in a considerable transfer of power to the masses, but in that case the powerful could not realize enormous profits unless they paid the masses to operate the industrial machinery. Will the masses find a way to use the power of the computer to strengthen their position even though they are no longer economically necessary? Will the powerful use the computer to prevent an increasingly disaffected population from exploding into violence? Much as we would like to believe that the intrinsic dynamics of the computer revolution will inevitably lead to economic justice, it seems more likely that those involved in computerization decisions (management and labor, government and citizens, computer professionals and computer users) will have to consciously and innovatively create a form of computerization that will result in a just distribution of the benefits of the computer revolution.

The Information Superhighway

John G. Nellist and Elliott M. Gilbert

After a brief explanation of its beginnings, John G. Nellist and Elliott M. Gilbert explain the many systems and services that make up the information superhighway. At each level, they show the changes it has brought and the benefits it offers, which include time and cost savings, customer satisfaction, and reduction in traffic and travel. Nellist is a consultant for Sarita Enterprises Ltd. in Canada. Gilbert, a consultant for Communication Systems and Services in California, holds nine patents. Both have received numerous awards for contributions in technology.

Much of the planned seamless global telecommunications network that we have begun to call the Information Superhighway is in place now and almost all of us use some part of it every day. Plain old telephone service (POTS) is something we all use to call within buildings or across town or perhaps to neighboring towns that are in our local calling area. . . . The communication facilities that provide POTS are one part of the Superhighway. . . .

When we call other cities we extend our use of the Superhighway to long distance networks in addition to local access. Prior to deregulation in 1982, long distance service within the United States was provided by AT&T. Since deregulation, it has been provided by special common carriers like Sprint, MCI, and AT&T. The Telecommunications Act of 1996 allows the telephone operating companies and the cable TV companies to compete for this business. In other countries in the world, networks are in place and internetworking technology has been developed to implement seamless international communications so that international calls can be direct-dialed and connections made almost instantaneously.

So, what does the world do with the tremendous band-width already installed and increasing daily in the fiber optic cables, satellites, cellular radios, and hybrid fiber/coax local distribution systems? What types of services will travel over the Superhighway? What are the current applications for the services, and what applications do we see for the future?

Types of Communications Services

The ITU-T [Consultative Committee on International Telegraphy and Telephony, now ITU-T] Study Group 18 (SGXVIII) has classified broadband communications services that could be supported by B-ISDN [Broadband Integrated [fax] Services Digital Network], which will be part of the Superhighway. Their classifications may be applied to telecommunications in general and are useful for contemplating the types of information that will flow over the Superhighway and the telecommunications media and technology that will be required to transport it.

The ITU-T considers two broad classifications: *interactive services* and *distribution services*. Interactive services provide two-way information exchange between points on a network, such as communications between two subscribers or between a subscriber and a database. Most of the information transfer consummated through the Internet is supported by interactive services.

The distribution services classification is divided into two subclassifications: distribution services without user individual presentation control, which are basically broadcast services such as broadcast television and radio, cable TV, and satellite TV; and distribution services with user individual presentation control, which allow the user to select the type of information of interest and control the start and order of the presentation. . . .

The Internet

Many consider the Internet to be the Information Super-highway. It is a vast global collection of networks that can

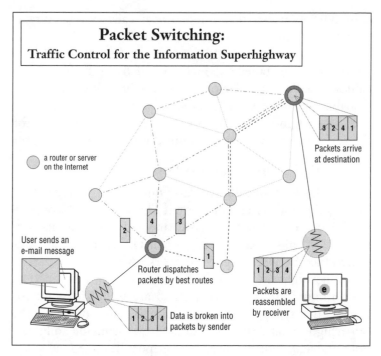

Packet Switching:
Traffic Control for the Information Superhighway

a router or server on the Internet

Packets arrive at destination

User sends an e-mail message

Router dispatches packets by best routes

Packets are reassembled by receiver

Data is broken into packets by sender

provide access to worldwide information sources. Users access the Internet through local service providers to reach content providers, such as databases and news and information sources. The backbone connections to the many networks of the Internet are made through the infrastructure of the long distance service providers.

So, the Internet may evolve to be the Superhighway or may simply remain part of it. What is important is the evolution of a seamless network that can provide a pathway that will satisfy the requirements of all of the telecommunications applications that now exist and those projected for the future.

Some of the applications use Internet pathways; many do not, rather, they use the transmission facilities of the telecommunications service providers or those of their own private networks directly. . . .

Business and the Internet

Business and commerce may be one of the largest applications of the Superhighway, and much of the use is through the Internet. The World Wide Web is one of the fastest growing uses of the Internet, with Web page growth estimated at 1,000% a year. The Web is a medium that is an advertising instrument, an information distribution agent, a means of generating sales leads, and an organization promotion vehicle. Companies that advertise on Web pages generate revenue through on-line orders for products and also realize savings from operations. For instance, requests for mailed information can be reduced considerably by allowing the information to be downloaded directly from the Web site. Other companies have found that the Web site can reduce the number of incoming toll-free 800 calls. Requests for pricing can go directly to an agent who can answer the request by e-mail. . . .

The Future Information Superhighway

Visible on the horizon of systems and device development, in addition to the developments already mentioned, are personal satellite telephones weighing 1 pound or less, personal lifetime telephone numbers that will be valid any place on the globe, radio receivers for Global Positioning Satellite information that will show the users their exact location, networks of low Earth orbit satellites that will allow mobile telephones to be reached any place on Earth, and e-mail desk telephones that will have internal storage of messages. Many other services that are beyond our imaginations today will be developed.

Artificial Intelligence Is Useful for Analyzing Complex Data

Fred Williams

Fred Williams explains artificial intelligence and analyzes its use for evaluating and selecting stocks in the investment community. Artificial intelligence programs are nontraditional; AI can evaluate variables, look for patterns, and offer suggestions based on analysis of patterns. Williams argues that because AI can handle more variables at one time and make faster calculations than humans can and because AI can learn from mistakes and change, it is likely to become more widely used in the investment business as the market becomes more complex. Williams is a freelance writer. He writes frequently about computer and business topics.

A Wall Street adage says that stock traders, given a choice, would rather have more luck than more market insight.

But a small group of highly specialized money managers using artificial intelligence programs believe that more insight is better. Their computers, they say, can analyze and pick stocks better than humans can by considering more variables on more stocks than a human ever could—and the computers learn from their mistakes.

Money managers have been slow to adopt artificial intelligence to select stocks, and consultants don't yet have the managers who do use artificial intelligence on their radar screens, largely because they don't fit into any convenient style boxes. But firms as large as Fidelity Investments Inc., Boston, are testing the waters, along with small specialized firms such as NeuWorld Financial, San Diego; and Advanced Investment Technologies, Clearwater, Fla. AIT is part of Boston-based State Street Global Advisors' global alliance of niche asset managers, a joint venture with Dutch pension fund ABP, Heerlen, Netherlands. No matter the size, all are hard at work trying to persuade institutional investors that AI is indeed the next new thing.

One of Several Tools

Fidelity's quantitative group is using AI "as one of several techniques" for stock selection in its $3.2 billion Disciplined Equity, $1.3 billion Stock Selector and $62 million Techno-Quant Growth funds, according to a spokesman. The group uses AI along with traditional fundamental stock analysis and other quantitative tools, he said.

Artificial intelligence systems also could get a shot in the arm if the California Public Employees' Retirement System, Sacramento, selects NeuWorld as part of its emerging manager program. CalPERS is committing up to $4 billion for emerging managers to run and investing another $80 million in equity positions in the firms (*Pensions & Investments*, Jan. 10, 2000).

NeuWorld is one of four firms under consideration for funding, said Hilda Ochoa, president of Strategic Investment Management Partners Inc., Washington, one of two firms hired by CalPERS to conduct due diligence on prospective managers for inclusion in the program. A decision is likely to be made within six months, she said.

The Way AI Works

A simplistic view of AI—which is widely used in the insurance, meteorology, engineering and aerospace industries, and by the military—is that it is an advanced computer program that can evaluate all of the variables it can be fed, looks for patterns and makes recommendations based on its analysis of those patterns. The complicated explanation is that it uses neural networks, genetic algorithms and fuzzy logic to evaluate non-linear combinations of data too subtle for the human brain or conventional computers to absorb.

Unlike traditional computer systems, which are programmed, AI uses neural networks to recognize and analyze patterns in data and develops models through learning rather than programming. It was AI that guided cruise missiles through the streets of downtown Baghdad during the Gulf War in 1991.

"It's quantitative in the sense that we use computers," said Barry Hippensteel, portfolio manager at NeuWorld, "But traditional quant shops use expert systems and linear calculations. They are fixed systems built to apply human rules and weightings programmed into them in selecting stocks. . . . A true AI system is like a baby. When it is created, it knows nothing. It starts to learn and to change itself when it's wrong. It remembers what is right and corrects itself."

Added Credibility

New York–based Standard & Poor's new Neural Fair Value 20 Portfolio makes its fair-value ranking system "more sensitive to prevailing market conditions," said Andre Archambault, research director in the S&P equity services division. Its creation also lends credibility to the use of artificial intelligence in the investment community.

NeuWorld's Mr. Hippensteel is almost evangelical in his quest to persuade the investment world that AI is better than people at evaluating stocks, and will get even better in the future.

"Using AI compresses time. We use price as one of 116 different variables in monitoring 4,000 domestic stocks, but we are more interested in understanding all the data in a pattern. The computer does more than 700 million calculations per month. Impossible for a human analyst. It is child's play for neural networks," he said.

A typical Wall Street analyst covers 30 to 40 stocks and uses fewer than 10 variables. Any more than that, he said, and "they start to break down."

The computer carves the universe into five categories based on its view of the stocks. NeuWorld is so confident, it claims that 90% of the stocks on its buy list will be up over the next 12 months and only 10% will be losers. On its website, www.ai-stocks.com, for example, among its top stock picks are: EchoStar Communications Corp., with an expected 12 month return of 101% with an 11% probability of being a loser. Others are Alltel Corp., with an expected return of 99% and a 10% probability of loss; AT&T Corp., 96% and 9%; Micron Technology Inc., also 96% and 9%; and Intel Corp., 85% and 5%.

Still Learning

A mock portfolio NeuWorld has been managing for CalPERS has shown mixed results, but the computer is still learning, said Mr. Hippensteel. The portfolio was up 26.7% in 1999, compared with the 21% gain for the S&P 500. In 2000, a rough year by any measure, the portfolio was down 25.9%, compared with the S&P's decline of 9.1%. A revised system, called Eagle 12, has shown improved results. Between Dec. 1, 2000, and May 1, Eagle 12 gained 12.1% while the S&P declined 4.1%.

Mr. Hippensteel said the NeuWorld approach is designed to do better over longer periods because of its capacity to learn.

"AI has the ability to look at the big picture, faster and more in depth than any human," he said. "That leads to solving problems that Wall Street has been trying to do for a long time."

That's not to say that AI never makes a mistake, he said, "but it never makes the same mistake twice. . . . AI learns how to change itself when it is wrong."

While NeuWorld follows the stock selection process of its AI system faithfully, other firms use it as a quantitative tool.

S&P's Mr. Archambault said the AI system he developed uses consensus earnings estimates as one of 12 variables in its analysis of 2,000 stocks. The portfolio consists of the 20 stocks identified as having the greatest potential for price appreciation over six to 12 months. The portfolio was up 15.8% between Sept. 30, when it was introduced, and April 30, vs. a decline of 18.7% for the S&P 500, he said.

"It usually outperforms human (analysts and stock pickers)," he said. "People tend to fall in love with stocks."

Advanced Investment Technologies uses AI to manage

nearly $800 million in institutional assets and, unlike Neu-World, it leaves the final decision on whether to buy or sell in the hands of a human. AI purists say this practice defeats the purpose of using AI in the first place.

Doug Case, AIT president, said AI is a "tool" for solving problems. "Our perspective on AI is more pragmatic," said Mr. Case, who prefers the term "intelligent data analysis" to "artificial intelligence." "One problem is that the market-place has become much more competitive and complex. Now you have to do more. Since the 1990s the investment process is more quantitatively driven. Where we have gone is to top engineers working to find techniques that have been proven in the physical sciences. There is some art to devel-oping these systems. There needs to be some resident ex-pertise in designing them, someone who also understands the data."

AIT analyzes 3,000 stocks using a combination of techni-cal, fundamental and macro variables such as interest rates, inflation, risk premiums and valuation. The variables are an-alyzed using neural networks and genetic algorithms to de-velop portfolios. But, said Mr. Case, AIT also follows a rig-orous risk-management formula, and "we look at the stock before sending it to the trading desk."

He said consultants and plan sponsors are not jumping on the AI bandwagon because "it's often more difficult for some plans to use newer investment techniques . . . and consul-tants often don't want to recommend that their clients be the first into something."

The AI universe remains largely an anomaly in the con-sulting community, which classifies AI managers as quantita-tive. A spokeswoman for William M. Mercer Inc., Washing-ton, said the firm's investment consultants "don't have a lot to say on this topic, because we don't see a lot of it out there. We don't run across it a lot in our work."

Mr. Case said AI techniques should catch on in coming years because of the growing complexity of the markets, which will require more computing power and analysis to deal with information overload.

"In the 1980s the models couldn't do as much. But markets are getting more complex and we can do more now. You have to use the tools that can handle that complexity," said Mr. Case.

Lack of Understanding

Robert Boldt, former senior investment officer at CalPERS and now managing director at Pivotal Asset Management LLC, San Francisco, said, "most consultants don't have a clue about what it (AI) is and don't want to embarrass themselves. Rather than (consultants) leading clients into new areas, it's usually the other way around."

Mr. Boldt, who was responsible for the CalPERS emerging manager program and chief architect of the CalPERS hedge-fund strategy prior to his departure for Pivotal, an equity management firm specializing in emerging technology growth stocks, called NeuWorld staff "pioneers in many ways. They are out there talking about it and have put it on their website for everyone.

"They've done a lot of work and are gutsy enough to put it on the web. I say more power to them. AI systems take into account more data than humans can. It can structure and generate an investment portfolio. It can do it over and over and learns when it makes a mistake."

Artificial Intelligence May Aid the Study of Evolution

Carl Zimmer

Carl Zimmer describes initial experiments comparing computer-generated "life" forms with biological life forms. Digital computer programs, called Digitalia, have been shown to mutate and evolve in certain ways. Zimmer explains one experiment in which Digitalia shrank like viruses to a simpler form, another in which Digitalia accommodated new conditions in ways similar to the bacteria *E. coli*, and others in which Digitalia may be used to study biological complexity. Scientists, however, are mindful of the limitations of Digitalia when comparing it with life forms. Zimmer, a science writer, is author of *At the Water's Edge* and *Parasite Rex*.

Computer scientists and biologists are finding common ground in the evolution of artificial and natural organisms.

Do universal laws of evolution exist? There's no bigger question in biology, and none harder to answer. To discover a universal rule, you need more than a single case, and when it comes to life, we're stuck with a data set of one. All life on earth descends from a common ancestor, with every species storing its genetic information in DNA (or, in the case of some viruses, RNA). If scientists someday discover another form of life, perhaps lurking on a moon of Jupiter or in some distant solar system, they may be able to compare its evolution to our own and see if the two histories have followed the same playbook. But such an opportunity may be a long way off.

In 1992 the eminent biologist John Maynard Smith declared that the only way out of this quandary was to build a new form of life ourselves. "We badly need a comparative biology," he wrote. "So far, we have been able to study only one evolving system, and we cannot, wait for interstellar flight to provide us with a second. If we want to discover generalizations about evolving systems, we will have to look at artificial ones."

In the nine years since Maynard Smith's call, computer scientists have done their best to answer it. They've tried to create a menagerie of artificial life-forms, from self-replicating software to "intelligent" robots, and they've set off plenty of breathless hype in the process. Some claim, for example, that computer processing speeds are climbing so quickly that within fifty years, robots with superhuman intelligence will be walking among us. Neuroscientists have countered that brains are much more than just masses of neurons: they consist of complex networks that communicate with one another using dozens of chemical signals. Even the simplest of these networks can take decades to decipher. Just figuring out the system of thirty neurons that lobsters use to push food through their stomachs has taken more than thirty years and the collective labor of fifteen research teams. At that rate, millions of years could pass before scientists fully comprehend the workings of the 100 billion neurons that make up the human brain.

Scientists Create Digitalia That Evolve

But not all is hype and skepticism. Suitably humble experts on artificial life and suitably open-minded biologists are starting to work together. One promising collaboration is being led by Chris Adami, a physicist at the California Institute of Technology; Charles Ofria, a former student of Adami's who is now at Michigan State University; and Richard Lenski, a microbiologist at Michigan State. Building on pioneering work by Tom Ray (now at the University of Oklahoma), Adami and Ofria have created computer programs—digital creatures—that behave in remarkably lifelike ways. And working with Lenski, they've shown that these creatures, which they call Digitalia, evolve much the way biological life-forms do.

Each digitalian consists of a short program that can be run by a computer. The computer moves line by line through the program, methodically executing each command until it reaches the end, whereupon it loops back to the beginning and starts over. A program can reproduce by instructing the computer to make a copy of the program, and this duplicate then starts running on its own.

Adami and his colleagues conceive of the digitalia as organisms living on a two-dimensional plane divided up into thousands of cells. Each digitalian occupies a single cell, and when it reproduces, its offspring take up residence in the adjoining cells. Once a digitalian starts reproducing, its progeny can race across the plane like mold spreading over a slice of bread. (The researchers can watch their progress by means of a graphic display on a computer screen, although the screen itself isn't actually the habitat—there's no one-to-one correspondence between the pixels and the cells.)

Digitalia don't simply replicate; they also evolve. Every time a digitalian replicates, there's a small chance the copy will contain a mutation. Mutations in nature are random changes in a sequence of DNA; in the case of digitalia, mutations consist of certain kinds of random changes in a program. For example, the computer may copy part of a program twice instead of once or may switch one command for another.

As in the real world, most mutations are harmful to digitalia, inserting fatal bugs that prevent them from replicating. Other mutations have little or no effect, building up like junk through the generations. And some help digitalia replicate faster. Those so blessed come to dominate their artificial world, just as natural selection favors well-adapted biological life.

Both Digitalia and Viruses Shrink

Adami and his associates have found that their digitalia consistently evolve in certain ways—ways that are similar to what biologists see in real life. In one experiment, they created several different strains of digitalia and let them evolve. They found that these programs consistently shrank down to sleek, short sequences of commands—as few as eleven command lines in some cases—that carried the minimum amount of information necessary for replicating. It takes less time to copy a short program than a long one, so the shorter the program, the more quickly it can multiply.

In the 1960s Sam Spiegelman and his colleagues at the University of Illinois got a similar result when they studied the evolution of RNA viruses. They put viruses into a beaker and supplied them with all the enzymes they needed to replicate. Twenty minutes later, the researchers transferred some of the newly replicated viruses to a new beaker and let them replicate again. After a few rounds, the scientists waited only fifteen minutes each time, and then only ten minutes, and finally only five. By the end of the experiment, the viral RNA had shrunk to 17 percent of its initial size. The viruses evolved into such small versions of themselves because they could shed genes they had used to invade and commandeer host cells. These had become unnecessary and now only slowed down the RNA's replication. As with digitalia, the most successful viruses under these conditions were the simplest.

Some Digitalia "Eat" Numbers and Multiply Faster

Normally, however, life doesn't exist in a test tube, with all its needs taken care of by a technician. Organisms have to eat, or photosynthesize, or somehow consume the energy and matter around them. To make digitalia more lifelike, Adami and his colleagues require them to eat to survive. Numbers are their food.

Each organism is supplied with a random sequence of 1's and 0's. Just as some bacteria eat sugar and transform it into useful proteins, digitalia are required to read these numbers and transform them into meaningful outputs. With the right combinations of commands, for instance, they can determine whether three numbers in a row are identical, or they can turn a string of numbers into its opposite ("10101" becoming "01010"). The scientists reward the digitalia for evolving the ability to do these tasks. The programs of these lucky organisms start running faster, and as a result, they multiply faster.

Soon their numbers overwhelm the less capable digitalia.

Under these complex conditions, the digitalia don't turn into stripped-down creatures. Instead, they evolve from simple replicators into sophisticated data processors that can crunch numbers in complicated ways. Human programmers, of course, can also write programs to carry out these tasks, but sometimes the digitalia evolve versions that are unlike anything ever conceived by a human designer.

Someday this sort of evolution may produce new kinds of efficient, crash-proof software. But Adami and Ofria are not interested in the commercial possibilities of digitalia; they're too busy working with Richard Lenski, comparing their artificial life to biological life.

Scientists Compare Digitalia and *E. coli*

The partnership began after Lenski heard Adami give a talk about his digitalia. Adami showed the audience a graph charting the creatures' replication rate. The line on the graph rose for a while before reaching a plateau and then rose to still higher plateaus in a series of sudden jerks. Lenski was astonished. He and his colleagues had observed how *Escherichia coli* bacteria evolved over thousands of generations, acquiring mutations that helped them consume sugar more efficiently and reproduce faster. When Lenski had charted their evolution, he had found the same punctuated pattern that Adami identified. Digitalia and *E. coli* apparently had some profound things in common. The two teams of scientists joined forces in 1998.

Since then, they have found more similarities between digitalia and biological organisms. In 1995 Lenski and a student, Mike Travisano, ran an experiment to gauge the importance of chance, history, and adaptation to the evolution of bacteria. From a single *E. coli* they cloned twelve populations, which they regularly supplied with the simple sugar glucose. Over the course of 2,000 generations, all the colonies evolved, becoming better and better adapted to the glucose diet. Then Lenski's team switched the bacteria to a diet of a different sugar, maltose. Over the course of another 1,000 generations, the colonies adapted until they could grow almost as well on their new food.

But the evolution of the colonies was not just a simple story of adapting to food. Lenski and his colleagues also kept track of the size of the microbes as they adapted. Originally the colonies were identical, but by the time the scientists switched them from glucose to maltose, they had diverged into a range of different sizes. Then, as the bacteria adapted to their new diet, their size changed again. Some colonies changed from big to small, others from small to big. Overall, the researchers found, the bacteria's adaptation to their diet had nothing to do with their size change. Chance mutations could alter cell size with little effect on their fitness, that is, their success in survival and replication.

Adami and a student, Daniel Wagenaar, recently converted Lenski's experiment into one they could run with their computer creatures. They created eight copies of a single program, which they used to seed eight separate digitalia colonies. The organisms were rewarded for mastering a set of logical operations, but once they had become well adapted, the researchers changed the reward system so that an entirely different set of operations was favored—a digital version of switching from glucose to maltose.

Adami and Wagenaar observed that digitalia could evolve quickly and thrive in new conditions, just as *E. coli* had. They also monitored the length of the programs—a trait that proved relatively unimportant to their fitness, just as cell size was for the bacteria. Adami and Wagenaar found that the evolution of a program's length was determined mainly by its history and by chance mutations, rather than by the pressure to adapt.

These parallel experiments suggest, once again, that artificial and biological life evolve according to at least some of the same rules. When it comes to traits that experience intense natural selection—such as the mechanisms for finding food or crunching numbers—the end results may erase much of a trait's previous history. But in the case of traits that experience only weak selection—such as the size of a bacterium or the length of a computer program—chance mutations can send evolution off in unpredictable directions, and their effects can linger for a long time as historical vestiges.

One of the great attractions of digitalia is that they're so much easier to work with than biological life. You can create billions of different digitalia strains and watch them evolve for thousands of generations in a matter of hours. And every step of that complicated journey is preserved on a computer, instantly available for study—making it possible to ask questions about digitalia that can't be addressed in ordinary experiments.

Using Digitalia to Study Complexity

For example, biological evolution has produced structures and organisms of awesome complexity, from termite colonies to the human brain. But does this mean that evolution has been dominated by a steady trend of rising complexity over time? A long line of thinkers have claimed that it does; one recent example is Robert Wright, in his book *Nonzero: The Logic of Human Destiny*. Stephen Jay Gould, on the other hand, has argued that what some people may interpret as an overall trend toward complexity is really the random rise and fall of complexity in different branches of the tree of life.

Though fascinating, this debate has stalled because scientists have yet to settle on a definition of complexity in biology or on a way to measure its change. Complexity is not unique to biology, however. Mathematicians have found precise ways to measure the complexity of information, whether it's a picture of Jupiter transmitted by the Galileo probe or the sound of a friend's voice on the telephone. Since digitalia genomes are strings of commands—in other words, information—Adami and his associates have been able to adapt mathematical methods to measure digitalia complexity as well.

To gauge how much of the information in a digitalia program is vital to the organism's survival, the researchers mutate each command in the program in every possible way and then see whether the organism can still function. A program may be stuffed with useless commands and turn out to be quite simple; even if you tamper with a lot of its code, it will still function. But another program of the same length may turn out to be complex, using most of its commands in precise ways that don't tolerate much tinkering.

Following this method, Adami and his coworkers have measured the complexity of digitalia colonies as they've evolved through 10,000 generations. Overall, the complexity consistently rises until it levels off. Its ascent is jagged but is an ascent nevertheless. For digitalia, at least, evolution does have an arrow pointing toward greater complexity.

Study of Digitalia Has Limitations

As interesting as these results are, any application to biological life comes with some important caveats. For one thing, the scientists only measured the information that was contained in the digitalia programs, which is akin to biologists measuring the complexity of information encoded in a genome. There's no simple equation that enables a biologist to use genetic complexity to calculate the complexity of the things a genome creates.

Another caveat to bear in mind is that the complexity of digitalia increases in a fixed environment—that is, the rewards for processing data don't change. In the natural world, conditions are always changing, with an endless flow of droughts, floods, outbreaks of disease, and other life-altering events. Every time conditions change, genes that were specialized to deal with the old conditions become useless. The obsolete genes may mutate or even disappear, and in the process, the complexity of a species' genome dwindles. Only as the species adapts to new conditions may complexity increase again.

In the natural world, the arrow of complexity may get turned back too often to have any significant effect on long-term evolution. But just finding that arrow is an admirable start. Indeed, everything about digitalia is, at the moment, a start—the start of a new kind of science and just maybe the start of a new kind of life.

Chapter 2

Technology's Effects on Business and Industry

Turning|Points

IN WORLD HISTORY

Automating a Factory

Gerard H. Michaud and Richard Burda

Gerard H. Michaud and Richard Burda argue that automating the handling of data is a good way to automate a factory because this application can be implemented in steps and because it has less risk and greater flexibility. By collecting and automating the analysis of data about equipment, the specifications of the process, and the location and status of the materials, factory managers can streamline flow through the factory and ultimately provide the customer with better service. Michaud is an engineering manager at Kulicke & Soffa Industries. Burda is a factory operations analyst for Kulicke & Soffa Factory Systems Group.

Automation solutions should not be analyzed separately from the total production environment. While few automation solutions add value directly to the product, all affect the performance of the entire production system. Understanding and controlling the behavior and performance of this system is paramount to implementing a controlled process that satisfies the business objectives of the factory.

Several robotic material-handling products have been introduced for test, assembly, and packaging (TAP) in semiconductor manufacturing with limited acceptance and proliferation. . . .

Myriad choices are available to factory managers who need to base factory automation decisions on operational objectives of their factories. Most importantly, TAP factory automation can be implemented in increments, achieving an aggressive ROI [return on investment] at each step. This methodology is contrary to the widespread belief that a factory is not automated until it "looks like wafer fabs (manufacturing completely automated from beginning to end) that use robotic material-handling systems."....

The Choice Between Automating the Handling of Materials (AMH) or Data (ADH)

The path to factory automation starts with a split that affects the ability to modify or alter future tactical automation decisions. The choice is to commit immediately to automated material handling (AMH) or to take the incremental approach beginning with automated data handling (ADH)....

The ADH path provides many choices for implementation. There are many opportunities for improving factory performance through the elimination of paperwork and manual bookkeeping. These may involve data associated with the plant and process equipment, or data associated with material or components being processed. Corresponding to these path choices are investments in plant infrastructure and software tools. From a basic host computer that collects equipment or material data to a full factory manufacturing execution system (MES), these investments can be matched to the needs of data management at the area, cell, or factory level. Unlike AMH, the investment in ADH is incremental.

Two Paths of ADH: Data About Process and Equipment and Data About Material

Along the path of ADH is another key split: one path focuses on data about the process and equipment, the other on data about material being processed. The equipment data-handling path can lead to advances in equipment utilization, process consistency, and ultimately process control and recipe management. The material data-handling path, on the other hand, provides basic tracking information, routing, and work in process (WIP) control. The paths of equipment and material data may eventually merge, providing several alternate objectives of device traceability, automatic recipe verification and download, factory planning, scheduling, and adaptive test process changes based on real-time material information.

Factory managers are driven to improve their operations

via, for example, reduced cycle time, assembly cost and space utilization, and high equipment utilization. Several specific steps to factory automation can help satisfy these drives:

- equipment monitoring and performance reporting;
- process recipe verification and management;
- lot tracking and WIP monitoring and management;
- device traceability;
- adaptive final test protocols;
- factory-wide planning and scheduling; and
- automated material transfer.

Achieving each of these steps requires specific data sets from a variety of automation products integrated in a bottom-up solution. The investment made in these product sets will depend on what requirements are targeted in a particular TAP [test, assembly, and packaging] cell, line, module, or factory, and which path has been chosen for preceding steps.

Equipment monitoring, performance reporting [: data about equipment] Equipment monitoring and performance reporting means improving process-equipment performance via equipment data. ADH makes equipment data quickly and easily available, allowing the identification of opportunities for improvement.

Managers can use equipment data in many ways to improve performance. For example, real-time equipment status permits immediate dispatch of technicians at the onset of unscheduled downtime. . . .

Process recipe verification, management [: data about process] One of the fundamental challenges of TAP is maintaining an acceptable level of performance while assembling a wide variety of packages. Most TAP processing tools have a different process recipe for each product. The management of these recipes is a considerable task for any TAP factory. The objective for automating recipe management is to shorten equipment changeover time and to eliminate yield losses caused by running the wrong recipe. . . .

Off-line programming refers to writing recipes that can be downloaded by the host [computer] on an independent PC. This eliminates downtime while programming recipes on the equipment. More elegant systems can convert existing prod-

uct drawings from CAD (computer-aided design) programs
to recipes. This feature dramatically reduces the time required to write equipment recipes and improves accuracy. . . .

   Lot tracking, WIP monitoring [: data about material] Tracking semifinished material within a factory means identifying
and locating any part or component within a factory at a given

---

A Multi-Approach to Reducing Costs

*Managers of the New Balance Athletic Shoe Company have em-
ployed worker cooperation, along with automation, to make their
American factory more efficient, according to Joshua Kurlantzick
in an article in* U.S. News & World Report.

While most other shoe manufacturers have fled U.S. soil,
New Balance Athletic Shoe, a privately held manufacturer
based in Boston, is determined to stay, relying on automation and worker cooperation to keep it profitable. . . .

   To boost worker productivity, New Balance trains its
workers intensely, even enrolling them in 22-hour courses.
The firm also makes large capital investments in its U.S.
plants, including a massive, Hydra-like robot whose arms
swing wildly around the floor of New Balance's Boston factory, picking up shoe uppers, joining them with soles, and
placing them on conveyor belts to be packaged.

   New Balance is also switching from incentive wages,
based on the number of shoes workers produce, to hourly
rates. [Executive vice president of operations Herb] Spivak
says that hourly rates "allow staff to concentrate on training
and upgrading their skills, and to internalize that the competition is other plants, overseas, not other workers next to
them. Our workers really take it as a point of pride to constantly one-up foreign-based factories."

   Manufacturing here has one other advantage: Plants are
closer to retailers, so the firm can respond more quickly to
new footwear trends, saving money on brainstorming and
advertising new models.

Joshua Kurlantzick, "New Balance Stays a Step Ahead," *U.S. News & World
Report,* July 2, 2001, p. 34.

time. Specific advantages include: process or material quality problems, in support of continuous process improvement, can be isolated, identified, and fixed faster; and production line conversions or process changes can be phased in faster. . . .

This approach provides data about the identity and location of all coded material to a point of inquiry. Factory personnel generate information about the identity, quantity, location, and time period of use. The task of hunting down lot travelers [tracking ticket] to make periodic inventories of WIP takes less time. In addition, this knowledge of material identity and location can begin the process of managing the amount of WIP at each station. Identifying and correcting process bottlenecks that arise suddenly from unscheduled downtime events downstream is much quicker than with a paper-traveler system. . . .

WIP management [: data about material] WIP management is distinguished from lot tracking and WIP monitoring by the ability to control WIP levels within the factory, thereby implementing material flow control. Two things are required to add WIP management: knowledge of basic machine status and a method to inform operators when and where to move WIP. . . .

The primary benefit of material flow control through WIP management is cycle time reduction. Reducing WIP, cutting batch sizes, and using WIP levels to control the material flow reduces cycle time. Equally important is the reduction in cycle time variability. The ability to operate with short, predictable cycle times allows shorter quotable lead times to customers and an advantage over competitors. WIP management can also reduce or eliminate paper lot travelers on the factory floor because manual ID readers record the path of material as it moves through the process.

Device traceability [: data about material and process] Traceability of finished goods in the field refers to after-the-fact identification of the facility, materials, and processes used to manufacture the product. Because traceability relates only to identification of product after it leaves TAP, it is generally a customer requirement. The objective is to provide a product history in the event of field failure, to reduce product liability cost, and to minimize recall expenses. Reasons why traceability of material data is necessary include:

- the ability to record serial numbers of components or lots for warranty, field service, and recall use;
- the recording of what specific process tools, process recipes, and operators were on the production line when the product was manufactured; and
- the recording of data and lot codes for failure analyses of returned or recalled parts. . . .

Adaptive final test protocols [: data about material allows for improvement of process] The ultimate gain from ADH is to incorporate material information into downstream TAP processes to take advantage of a priori knowledge of the material by adjusting or adapting processing parameters, thereby saving time or improving quality. . . .

Factory-wide planning, scheduling After implementation of WIP management, higher-level factory improvements can accrue from the addition of production planning and real-time scheduling capabilities. In a production system with automated flow control, a scheduler can release lots into the system for processing and also select lots to be processed at each station.

By automating data systems, factory managers are able to streamline production flow, reduce costs, and ultimately provide better customer service.

Schedulers make decisions based on current factory status, including equipment status, WIP levels, order backlog, order due dates, and other information relevant to operations. This information is then put into mathematical models that consider the relative importance of different scheduling decisions. A scheduler outputs directives telling when to release and process each lot.

The scope of factory planning is larger than production scheduling. Factory planning software makes decisions regarding staffing, procurement, and subcontracting. . . .

Automated material handling Without material management software tools to direct an AMH transfer system, robot-based or linked equipment can only perform a limited function. This functionality—moving material from one process tool to another—has significant benefits: the elimination of labor and errors caused by mishandling or mixing WIP. . . .

If implemented without material management software tools, AMH systems cannot significantly improve product cycle time or reduce WIP levels. Robotic transfer times are often not much faster than a person. Getting material to a process station faster will not reduce the backlog at that station. Thus, the benefits of automated material transfer are not as pervasive as once perceived.

Conclusion [: selecting the right automation strategy] We suggest that incremental TAP automation implementation provides a migration path offering aggressive ROI with less risk than all-inclusive automation. Detailed knowledge of each factory is required to select one automation strategy over another. Today, there are many options for TAP factories to improve operations through large- and small-scale automation implementation.

Computers in Control of Modern Warfare

Gregory J.E. Rawlins

Gregory J.E. Rawlins analyzes the role of computers in modern weaponry and speculates on the future of warfare. He explains, for example, the cruise missile, ships and planes piloted by computers, and the cost of computerized war technology. Rawlins suggests that someday robots will replace soldiers and that competition among nations will accelerate to the point at which wars will be fought with software and hardware, with humans' role reduced to casualties. Rawlins teaches computer science at Indiana University in Bloomington. He is the author of *Compared to What: An Introduction to the Analysis of Algorithms* and *Slaves of Machines: The Quickening of Computer Technology.*

When most of us think of robots, it's usually as slow, dumb, unwieldy beasts slaving in factories, much as oxen slaved in fields generations ago. But robots aren't only in the factory, helping us make our cars; they're also on the battlefield, helping us make our wars. And they certainly aren't slow, dumb, and unwieldy.

During the 1991 Gulf War, America released 288 cruise missiles against Iraq; 80 percent of them hit their targets, with no loss of human pilots—at least, no American ones. Each missile delivered up to 450 kilograms of high explosives. They could just as easily have carried nuclear warheads.

A cruise missile is essentially a robotic bomber. It's like a piloted bomber, but better: It's smaller, cheaper, stealthier, and very precise. Its computers record exactly where it is at all times, thanks to radio contact with world-spanning satellites; and it has extensive electronic maps of where it's going. Like a bloodhound straining at the leash, it can be launched more than two thousand kilometers [1,240 mi] from its target and reach it to within a few meters. It could hit a garage door in Dallas from a rooftop in Los Angeles.

Flying at treetop level, it can turn corners, avoid obstacles, and fly through doorways. Its small size and low flight path lets it hide from enemy radars in the radar clutter near the ground. Even if detected, it's almost impossible to hit. Its next generation, to be deployed during this decade, will be smarter, stealthier, and faster and will peel off independently targeted smart missiles and bomblets as it flies.

Since each cruise missile has its own computer—and satellite links to establish its exact location—a cruise missile salvo can regroup in flight like a flight of deadly birds to hit its targets in precise sequences. The first wave usually destroys the foe's radar and surface-to-air missiles. Later waves mow down the installation itself—a missile complex, an air base, a command bunker. Next-generation missiles will adapt their targeting in flight as conditions on the battlefield change and as targets move around.

Today's cruise missiles cost about 1.3 million dollars each. Since much of that cost pays for sophisticated electronics, the price will drop as computer technology matures. A single American stealth bomber, on the other hand, costs hundreds of millions. And that's not counting the costs of employing several dozen mechanics per plane, training flight crews, and transporting many tons of fuel, munitions, and support equipment. It's certainly not counting the human and political cost of losing even a single pilot. Although nowhere near as adaptive, robot planes are cheaper and decidedly more expendable. It's clear where the future of air war lies.

Ships Operated from the Computer Control Center

Gone are the days when a captain could stand on a ship's bridge and see everything important through a pair of binoculars. Nowadays, a warship's radar extends at least a hundred kilometers in every direction—from four to ten times farther than simple binoculars. Nor does its vision go away at night or in fog. Nowadays, the captain's place isn't on the bridge, it's in the warship's computer nerve center.

A darkened room of glowing consoles and tiny blinking lights, the control room may as well be underground, far from the ship it commands. During war, the only physical feedback officers there get is the noise of departing missiles and the swaying of the room as the ship heaves through the swells.

For these officers, war has become a video game. Enemies are no longer ferocious warriors with teeth bared and weapons raised. They are blips on a phosphorescent screen with little symbols showing what a computer thinks they are. If the program controlling that computer is wrong, the information is wrong and the officers make mistakes. More often though, the emotionless computer is right but its displays are badly designed; and in the fever of war the officers are likely to misread the computer's messages. . . .

With the time to decide life-and-death matters sometimes reduced to seconds, we have less control. As computerized antiship missiles like the Exocet got better, ships started carrying computerized guns that can fire automatically on anything approaching the ship that looks like a missile. There's no longer time for John Wayne to smoke a meditative pipe as he plots an attack on the enemy's ships. Too many things happen too fast and too far away for warriors to make eyeball contact. As a result, mistakes happen.

On the other hand, mistakes always happen—particularly in the chaos of war. And perhaps human-computer systems make fewer mistakes today than unaided people did in the past. Unfortunately, because our systems are far more complex, powerful, and integrated, the consequences of today's mistakes can be far graver than yesterday's. When village waterwheels were our main source of power and bows and arrows our main weapons, a mistake in the way we use them couldn't affect that many of us. Things are different in an era of nuclear power stations and nuclear weapons. Blundering while hurling a spear is one thing; blundering while launching a space shuttle is another. . . .

Computers Replacing Humans in Air War

Thanks to computers, weapons are becoming smarter and more independent. Once upon a time, our weapons were so slow and inaccurate that we had to wait until we could see the whites of their eyes. Now we don't even have to wait until we can see their country, let alone their eyes.

Over half the cost of today's advanced warplanes goes into computers. With fire-and-forget long-range smart missiles, most aerial dogfights have become contests to see who has the best ones. Today's warplanes fight from ten to forty kilometers away—sometimes even from two hundred kilometers. Most advanced jet planes are simply unflyable without computer aid.

Warplanes are getting smarter too. They have sensors built right into their skin and they carry more and more competent computers, some of which understand and accept a few spoken commands, even when the pilot is under stress. Target-finding computers can pick out potential attack points hundreds of kilometers away at night and in bad weather. Still more computers track and relay target information to yet other computers that order the plane's missiles and guns to seek and destroy the targets. Other computers manage fuel consumption, check for hostile radar, continuously manipulate the warplane's numerous control surfaces for best flying, and plan the shortest and safest flight path.

Yet the present generation of fighter planes is not as good as it can be because pilots are fragile. Carrying a pilot today is like going to war with eggs in your pocket. Turns have to be wider and dives and climbs shallower than they could be. No such limits apply to the robotic antiaircraft missiles trying to blow the plane out of the sky. Further, during a dogfight, warplanes could be closing at over Mach 4—upwards of one and a half kilometers a second. With today's air-to-air missile range of around fifty kilometers, two pilots who detect each other from sixty-five kilometers away have less than ten seconds to decide what to do. And what's an eyeblink to us can be an eternity to a computer.

There's another reason we're vanishing from warplanes: We cost too much. It takes between five and ten million dollars to train a pilot. And the costs of a human crew add another one to five million dollars for extra space and weight (oxygen, extra fuel, seats, parachutes, and so on). In addition, warplanes are bigger, slower, heavier, and clumsier because of their human cargo. Having to carry a crew decreases an aircraft's weapons load and maneuverability, expands fuel needs and cost, reduces its range and speed, and vastly increases the human and political costs of losing even one. For all these reasons, pilots and weapons officers in today's advanced warplanes are an endangered species. They're on their way out, shouldered aside by lighter, cheaper, faster, more expendable, and more rugged silicon soldiers.

In the 1940s, heavy bombers needed a crew of twelve; by the 1950s, that dropped to six; by the 1970s, it was four; and by the 1980s, only two. In the decades to come, there will be one, and then—like cruise missiles—none. . . .

The High Cost of Advanced Technology

During wartime, advanced nations also use three-hundred-million-dollar air traffic and ground-surveillance aircraft. Each of these planes can replace the control tower of an entire major airport. They can track, identify, and disentangle over a thousand jets flying close together. Their radar can see small low-flying aircraft from three hundred kilometers away and large high-flying aircraft from six hundred kilometers away. Others can look down on a battlefield to track and identify every moving thing within five hundred square kilometers. For the first time in history, some military commanders can see, identify, and pinpoint everything on, below, and above the battlefield.

In future wars, aircraft might sprinkle tiny, cheap, and mobile noise, heat, light, radio, magnetic, and seismic detectors all over the battlefield. Commanders could then have a soldier's view, a tank's view, a pilot's view, and a satellite's view of a battle as it happens. Such technology could also give troops a nearly indestructible cellular-phone system. Orbiting satellites and other such technology are the eyes and ears of a modern military. Without them, modern armed forces are blind, deaf, mute, and lost. All are the result of the ever-increasing speed, power, and miniaturization of computers.

So, for a time, the fog of war is lifting—at least for a modern military facing a less-advanced one. But it will be back. Because all armed forces are keen to develop a means to jam, confuse, or destroy the current detection technology. Many of the secret satellites orbiting above are anti-satellites—intended to destroy other satellites in time of war. So future battlefields will inevitably become as confused as they were in [Prussian military analyst Karl von] Clausewitz's time [around 1850] and the first salvos of any future battle between modern nations will have to start in space.

In war, electronics can make the difference between life and death. A basic thirty-kilometer radar in your warplane might cost a quarter of a million dollars. Doubling the price can increase its accuracy and extend your sight to forty kilometers, letting you spot attackers sooner. Doubling the price again allows you to see seventy kilometers ahead, lets your radar guide your missiles, and gives you better tracking and safer low-altitude flying. Double the price yet again—to two million dollars—and you get vision out to almost two hundred kilometers and better ability to see through sophisticated electronic defenses. Similar escalations hold for the missiles you're about to fire and the warplane you're flying in.

Even the lowly bullet might eventually get its own computer. Every modern air, sea, or land warcraft needs computers—to help it sense its environment, target and deliver its weapons, move itself around, and support its crew. Electronics goes into satellites, planes, helicopters, missiles, ships, submarines, tanks, armored vans, artillery, and on, and on, and on.

All those computers cost money. America's newest attack submarine, for instance, costs 2,100 million dollars. And its newest stealth bomber costs another 2,200 million. Such enormous quantities of money give rich nations a significant military edge. The more they spend, the safer their troops are. Every commander who has to lead troops into battle and be held responsible for their lives wants the best equipment money can buy—and no one wants to tell the taxpayers that they're trading today's dollars for tomorrow's body bags. . . .

Modern war is definitely not for the poor. During the 1980s, America alone spent two million dollars on its armed forces. Worldwide, weapons costs alone now make up about half of all military spending, and more than a third of that goes for electronics. Even though the Cold War is over, overall military spending on electronics is rapidly approaching 20 percent of the world's military budgets. All countries combined presently spend around a million dollars a year on their armed forces. (That's more than all warring nations spent in 1944, the year of heaviest fighting during the Second World War.) Military electronics alone will thus soon consume almost two hundred thousand million dollars a year—and the amount can only increase. Nobody wants to lose the next war. . . .

Escalation of Computer Competence

The common thread through all of this change is the relentless escalation of computer competence. To shoot down bothersome aircraft, one side develops antiaircraft missiles. To destroy those missiles, the other side develops antimissile missiles. To confuse the antimissiles, the first side develops jammers, scramblers, and decoys. To cut through that interference, the other side develops smarter missiles. To reduce the human cost of aircraft losses, the first side develops robot planes. And so it goes, on and on, in a never-ending upward spiral. . . .

The greatest change in war in the past few decades has been the speed of improvement in machine competence. Because computers now control everything in sight, a weapon's usefulness is determined not just by its physical characteristics, but also by the capabilities of its computer programs. Immaterial computer programs inside weapons are far easier to change than the weapons themselves. For example, today's Patriot missile is essentially the same as it was in the 1980s, but its software has been significantly enhanced. Even during the short Gulf War, it went through three upgrades.

The shift toward software development will drastically change weapons deployment and enhancement cycles. It used to take ten to fifteen years for anything to really change on the battlefield, simply because a decade or more was needed to design, prototype, manufacture, and deploy new weapons. Now that time can sometimes be cut to a year or less—in extreme cases to a few months—because the hardware isn't changing—the software is. . . .

The Future War Machines

What might war become thirty to fifty years hence? As far as anyone knows—at least publicly—no weapon has yet gone to war completely on automatic, although several that could do so already exist. It used to be that cold steel and a stout heart were all you needed to win a battle. No longer.

Once, long ago, guns were single-shot. It took a long time to load and fire one bullet. A long, slow, and complex human process preceded the trigger pull, and a short, fast, and simple mechanical sequence followed it. The human had complete control of the machine. By the 1870 Franco-Prussian War, however, pressing the trigger of the first machine guns could result in the release of over a hundred bullets a minute. By the turn of the century, guns had evolved from dripping faucets into gushing firehoses.

It was still true that a human decision preceded pressing the trigger; barring a malfunction, nothing could happen without that decision. Even so, the human labor and decision-making involvement dropped dramatically. The machine now executed a much longer, much faster, and much more complex sequence of mechanical actions. After taking the initial decision, the human was much less in control of the machine.

What works for machine guns works for everything else about war. On the battlefield, every military commander must see what's going on, decide what to do, do it, then evaluate its effect. That see-decide-act cycle must be complete before the enemy completes its own cycle or the commander loses the initiative, and perhaps the war. Any edge in speed must be exploited.

Over the next forty years or so, under the mutagenic pressure to react faster and faster, automation may progress to the point where computers control entire ships (or tanks or planes). Today, in immediate combat, they control, or can control, weapons and sensors. Tomorrow, to speed up responses even further, they might control propulsion, maneuver, and life-support systems. Next week, they might control tactics. Of course, overall strategy will still remain with human commanders. It will still be true that, barring malfunction, the initial decision to go to deadly force will be a human one. Once that choice is made, though, each warcraft might execute a vast and intricate sequence of very fast actions, adapting its responses second-by-second.

Of course, none of that can happen in twenty years, perhaps not even in thirty; in thirty years we probably won't yet have cheap machines good enough to replace many soldiers on the battlefield. Thirty to fifty years from now, however, machines are likely to be quite capable warriors—and quite cheap. Time is on their side.

When America was testing the first stealth fighter in 1983, for instance, some computer engineers programmed it to fly itself from takeoff to landing. The plane executed all turns, minimized its exposure to detected radar sites, and even simulated dropping its bombs. Its pilot was merely along for the ride. Such advanced planes are unflyable without computer aid anyway; they're already essentially flying computers. They still have pilots for two reasons. First, human pilots, despite their enormous costs, often can handle unexpected situations; they're still far, far more adaptable than machine pilots. Second, no present-day air general would approve funding for an aircraft specifically designed not to need a pilot. Today's generals grew up in an age when that was unthinkable. Even suggesting doing away with human pilots was enough to doom your career. . . .

Aviation has already begun to hit the limits of human performance, but conditions will shortly worsen for infantries as well. Although robot tanks, for instance, have big problems with maintenance and refueling, each crew member eliminated makes them—like warplanes—that much cheaper, smaller, and more expendable. Today, they typically carry three people. In a few decades, they may carry none.

Rich nations are now deploying flying and swimming robots. Twenty to thirty years from now, they will be fielding walking, driving, and crawling robots carrying guns and bombs—big ones. Ten years after that, the face of war will have changed forever. War is now beginning to cycle at electronic speeds, and we aren't fast enough to keep making all the decisions. So, inevitably, we'll shunt more and more decision making to computers. Eventually, the only thing we may decide about any warcraft is whether or not to deploy it. Once we do, it may find its own targets and seek to destroy them without our intervention.

The Place of Humans in Future Warfare

In one extreme version of the possible future, the only military decision we humans make comes at the beginning of the war, in the choice to go to deadly force. Once we make that decision, there may be savage and unyielding machine conflict until one side or the other is destroyed. In some sense we will still be in control: Without our initial decision there would be, barring malfunction, no carnage. Still, considering the vast difference between our sole—albeit momentous—choice and the myriad layers of contingent choices our future machines may make, we'll have little real control. Our choices will be reduced to a very narrow range, while the consequences may be drastic and widespread.

For, of course, wars won't ever be only wars of machines. As long as we make the policy, there'll be no point having a war if only machines are destroyed. Each side will do its damnedest to hurt the other folks—not just their machines. That, at least today, is what wins wars. So the nation putting more human capital on the battlefield in future wars will merely be giving its enemy hostages to fortune.

Yesterday, we had armed soldiers. Today, we have manned weapons. Tomorrow, we may have autonomous warcraft. But we'll still be doing all the dying.

Chapter 3

Society in the Computer Age

Turning | Points
IN WORLD HISTORY

Computer Literacy for the Twenty-First Century

Michael B. Eisenberg

To Michael B. Eisenberg, computer literacy is more than the skillful use of computer technology; it involves thinking and creative problem solving. He describes a process, called the Big6, which combines the teaching of computer skills with high-quality instruction in content subjects. He illustrates the Big6 process with assignments in social studies and English and summarizes the major features of effective computer literacy education. Eisenberg, director of the Information School at the University of Washington in Seattle, is the coarchitect of the Big6 Skills Approach.

Learning to use technology is a clear goal in K–12 education today, and schools worldwide are scrambling to add hardware, software, and connectivity and to infuse computer technology into the instructional program. We're making progress in terms of the computer-student ratio, the installation of local networks, and the level and speed of Internet connectivity.

The Meaning of "Computer Literate"

We also see progress in defining what it means to be "computer literate," i.e., it is more than simply being able to operate a computer. First, educators are realizing that it's not just computers that we want students to be able to use. We want them to be literate in using the full range of information technologies—productivity tools, communications capabilities, information resources and systems, hand-held de-

Excerpted from "Beyond Bells and Whistles: Technology Skills for a Purpose," by Michael B. Eisenberg, *Multimedia School*, May 2001. Copyright © 2001 by Information Today, Inc. Reprinted with permission.

vices, and more. Second, the focus is shifting from "teaching computing in a separate class located in a computer lab" to "students learning to use the full range of information technology for a purpose as part of the subject area curriculum."

We want students to know more than a particular set of commands or even how to use a particular type of software. We want students to use technology flexibly and creatively. We want them to be able to size up a task, recognize how technology might help them to fulfill the task, and then use the technology to do so.

Helping students learn to apply technology in these ways requires a change in the way computer skills are traditionally taught in school. It means moving from teaching isolated "computer skills" to teaching integrated "information and technology skills." Integration means infusing technology in the curriculum. For example, instead of holding isolated lab sessions on how to use PowerPoint, students learn PowerPoint when they work on a project in social studies, science, or language arts. Integrating technology into content areas is motivating—it helps students see the relevance of the computer skills that they learn.

But this is not enough! Students also need to see how technology boosts their abilities, how it enables them to be more effective and efficient in tasks such as these:

> figuring out what they need to do, finding and using information, presentations, and reports.

The context for this type of integration is "process" (as opposed to "content"); the most widely used model to represent "process" is the Big6 Skills model of information problem-solving, which I developed together with my colleague Robert Berkowitz.

The Big6, a Process Model That Teaches Problem Solving

The Big6 is a process model that helps people of all ages solve information problems. From practice and study, we found that successful information problem-solving encompasses six stages (see Figure 1).

Figure 1: The Big6 Skills

1. Task Definition
    1.1 Define the information problem.
    1.2 Identify information needed in order to complete the task (to solve the information problem).

2. Information-Seeking Strategies
    2.1 Determine the range of possible sources (brainstorm).
    2.2 Evaluate the different possible sources to determine priorities (select the best sources).

3. Location and Access
    3.1 Locate sources (intellectually and physically).
    3.2 Find information within sources.

4. Use of Information
    4.1 Engage (e.g., read, hear, view, touch) the information in a source.
    4.2 Extract relevant information from a source.

5. Synthesis
    5.1 Organize information from multiple sources.
    5.2 Present the information.

6. Evaluation
    6.1 Judge the product (effectiveness).
    6.2 Judge the information problem-solving process (efficiency).

People go through these stages—consciously or not—when they seek or apply information to solve a problem or make a decision. It's not necessary to complete these stages in a linear order, and a given stage doesn't have to take a lot of time. We have found that in almost all successful problem-solving situations, all stages are completed.

The Big6 approach to teaching information and technology skills has been widely adopted around the world. Used in thousands of K–12 schools, higher-education institutions, and corporate and adult training programs, this information problem-solving process is applicable whenever people need and use information.

The Big6 Process Has Broad Benefits

In addition to considering the Big6 as a process, another useful way to view it is as a set of basic, essential life skills. These skills can be applied across situations—to school, personal, and work settings. These skills are applicable to all subject areas across the full range of grade levels. Students use the skills whenever they need information to solve a problem, make a decision, or complete a task.

The Big6 provides the framework for learning and applying technology. Individual information and technology skills take on new meaning when integrated within the Big6, and students develop true "computer literacy" because they have genuinely applied various computer and technology skills as part of the learning process.

In a recent survey of Big6 users, educators stated that using the Big6 helps to ease students' anxiety when they face an information problem or a research assignment. The Big6 gives students a way to focus and to feel confident when they approach assignments and projects.

Moving from teaching isolated computer skills to helping students learn integrated information and technology skills is not just a good idea. It's essential if we are to put students in a position to succeed in an increasingly complex and changing world. "To thrive in today's world and tomorrow's workplace, American students must learn how to learn, learn how to think, and have a solid understanding of how technology works and what it can do" (CEO Forum on Education & Technology, 1997). In my view, the CEO Forum is saying that being able to use computers is not enough. Students must be able to apply computer skills to real situations and needs; they must be able to identify information problems and be able to locate, use, synthesize, and evaluate information in relation to those problems.

There are many good reasons for moving from teaching isolated computer skills to teaching integrated information and technology skills. Technology is changing at a breathtaking pace and will continue to do so for the foreseeable future. In a speech at the 1997 National Educational Computing Conference in Seattle, [Microsoft's Bill] Gates stated that computing power has increased 1 million times over the past 20 years and will likely do so again in the next 20 years!

A million times more powerful!! Will learning isolated specific skills such as keyboarding, word processing, or even Web searching suffice? Clearly not. Will learning to use whatever technologies come along to boost our abilities within the overall information problem-solving process suffice? Absolutely.

Technology Is Incorporated into the Process

It's actually relatively easy to view technology from a Big6 perspective.

Let's take a typical basic technology: pencil and paper. In Big6 terms, how can a pencil and paper help us be more productive? Clearly, a pencil and paper boosts our ability to synthesize, organize, and present information (Big6 #5).

What are the electronic equivalents of a pencil and paper—the tools that help us even more to synthesize? Clearly, there's word processing. There's also desktop publishing, HyperStudio, PowerPoint, and other presentation software programs. All these are used to organize and present information (Big6 #5).

Here's another basic technology: a phone book. The phone book is an aid for Big6 #3—location and access. What are the electronic technology equivalents to the phone book? There are the online or CD-ROM bibliographic databases, Web browsers, and search engines.

Other technologies can be viewed in this way. Similar to books, full-text databases, CD-ROM encyclopedias, and other electronic resources are part of an effective information-seeking strategy (Big6 #2) and are read, viewed, or listened to for information (Big6 #4). When a face-to-face meeting isn't possible, e-mail is highly useful for linking students with their teachers or with other students for task-definition activities (Big6 #1) and later for evaluation (Big6 #6). And more and more students are learning to take notes and extract information by using the copy-and-paste functions in word-processing software.

When integrated into the information problem-solving process, these technological capabilities become powerful information tools for students. Figure 2 provides a summary of how some of today's technologies fit within the Big6 process.

Figure 2: Computer Capabilities and the Big6	
Word processing	Synthesis (writing) Use of Information (note-taking)
Spell/grammar checking	Evaluation
Desktop publishing	Synthesis
Presentation/multimedia software	Synthesis
Electronic spreadsheets	Synthesis
Online library catalog	Location and Access
Electronic magazine index	Location and Access Use of Information
Full-text electronic resources	Information-Seeking Strategies Use of Information
Brainstorming software	Task Definition
Copy-paste (in various programs)	Use of Information

Integrating technology instruction with the Big6 provides a context for technology skills instruction. It also helps students learn to apply technology flexibly and creatively.

Sample Assignments Using Big6

I talked above about the importance of two contexts—the Big6 process and the subject area classroom curriculum—to effective Big6 Skills instruction. This is particularly true for teaching technology skills. You avoid teaching technology skills in isolation when you combine them with this process and with real subject-area curriculum and assignments.

Social Studies. For example, a 9th grade class is studying regions of the Far East and comparing various features (e.g., geography, population, industry, and social attributes). The assignment is to create a comparative chart that highlights differences and similarities.

As students go through the work for the assignment, they engage in various stages of the Big6 process. The teacher recognizes that this might be a good opportunity to teach technology and the process itself. She arranges with the library media specialist for the students to learn about electronic searching for books in various electronic resources (Big6 #3, Location and Access). The students will also search the Web and compare what they find in terms of quality, amount of information, and time and effort.

The teacher also speaks to the technology teacher about possible programs to help the students create charts (Big6 #5, Synthesis). The technology teacher recommends a draw/paint program and schedules the class for a special lesson.

This is a powerful example of the integration of technology, the Big6, and curriculum. Students are learning to use technology as part of the information problem-solving process to perform better in classroom curriculum.

English. An English class is studying American literature. Working in groups, the students are to create a formal report on the historical context of a novel that they selected. The students brainstorm possible sources, and one group decides that talking to someone who is an expert in history and American literature is a good idea; perhaps this person is teaching at a university (Big6 #2, Information-Seeking Strategies). However, they realize they have no way of getting to a university or anywhere else by themselves (Big6 #3). Their teacher suggests they send an e-mail message to the library media specialist asking what to do. They do so, and she suggests conducting the interview through the Internet, either by e-mail or chat.

But where can they find a likely university and the e-mail address of someone there who teaches this subject (Big6 #3)? The students realize they can use a Web search engine to locate various universities, which probably include names of staff.

Over the next few days, the students make contact with a

university professor who agrees to answer their questions via e-mail. The students e-mail the questions and are excited when they get a response in 3 days. They copy and paste from the e-mail message into a word-processing document and note the name of their contact, e-mail address, and dates of the e-mail exchanges.

Technologies incorporated in this example include the use of a messaging or e-mail program, Web search engine, Web browser, and a word-processing program. The copy-paste function from e-mail is also an important skill for the students to learn. Another twist to this assignment would be to use multimedia presentation software to create and present the report instead of the traditional written format (Big6 #5).

The Results of Integrating Technology with Quality Instruction

When you reflect on integrating technology skills into teaching and learning, you realize that it is not necessary to change the fundamentals of quality instruction or the information problem-solving perspective that is at the heart of this approach. The implementation of technology through the Big6 works in the following ways:

- It develops students' problem-solving, complex-thinking, and information-management abilities.
- It enables students to become comfortable with technology and to understand that the technologies are valuable tools to help them perform their work.
- It focuses students' attention on using technologies as tools to extend knowledge and to individualize learning.
- It develops an active participatory learning process in which students become self-directed learners.
- It facilitates integrating technology across all grades and into all disciplines.
- It assists teachers to change their roles from presenters of information to "learning coaches" who offer tools and advice.
- It helps teachers introduce technology and to have students use technologies even if the teachers aren't experts themselves.

Implementing technology within the Big6 process is easy, direct, and powerful; it also encourages classroom teachers, library media specialists, and technology teachers to collaboratively design instruction that can intentionally create challenging and exciting learning experiences. Such opportunities expand the scope of new technology use by all students.

Training Improves Negative Attitudes Toward Computers

Claudia Orr, David Allen, and Sandra Poindexter

Claudia Orr, David Allen, and Sandra Poindexter conducted a study based on the assumption that many people
have negative attitudes toward computers. Their study
was designed to test the hypothesis that taking a course in
computer literacy can improve attitudes. Using 214 university student subjects, the authors discovered that students with prior computer experience had fewer negative
attitudes at the beginning of the course. By the end of the
course, the students who originally had had little or no experience displayed attitudes like those of students with
prior experience. Therefore, the authors conclude, computer literacy courses are important for educational institutions and for the workplace. All three authors teach at
Northern Michigan University in Marquette. Orr teaches
communications and computer applications; Allen teaches
quantitative analysis; and Poindexter teaches programming and systems analysis.

Computer competency is no longer a skill to be learned
only by students majoring in technology-related fields. All
individuals in our society must acquire basic computer literacy to function successfully. Despite the widespread influx
of technology in all segments of our society, the literature
often report high levels of anxiety and negative attitudes
about using computers. Monitoring the computer attitudes
and developing an understanding of the variables that affect
computer attitudes will assist educators and adult trainers in
providing appropriate learning experiences in which learn-

ers can succeed. This study examined the relationship between computer attitude and experience, demographic/education variables, personality type and learning style of 214 students enrolled in a university computer literacy course.

The Nature and Extent of the Problem

It has become apparent that computer competency is necessary not only for citizens to function efficiently on a personal level in our society, but to develop, advance and succeed in their professional lives. End-user computing (computing skills needed to complete tasks) has emerged as a significant issue affecting organizations. As [researchers] Torkzadeh and [Irma E.] Angulo (1992) caution, "the success of this end-user computing is dependent on the user's acceptance and commitment."

Unfortunately, despite the increasing use of computers in schools, homes, and workplaces across the United States, research continues to report high levels of anxiety, resistance and poor attitudes toward computers among students in higher education who are preparing for professional careers as well as those employees already well established in the workplace. In 1993 researchers Rosen and Well estimated that technophobia afflicted as many as one-third of the 14 million college students in the country ([Thomas J.] DeLoughry, 1993). A study supported by Dell Computers concluded that 55% of Americans suffer from some degree of technophobia (S. Williams, 1994). [John W.] Ostrowski, [Ella P.] Gardner, and [Magda H.] Motawi (1986) conducted a study to determine the extent of end-user attitude problems; more than 50% of the respondents indicated observing computer attitude problems, with anxiety occurring most often. A meta-analysis of computerphobia research led [L.R.] Rosen and [P.] Maguire (1990) to conclude that one fourth to one third of all people—college students, businesspeople, and the general public—may be classified as "computerphobic." They also indicate that an additional segment of the population is uncomfortable with computers and will avoid them whenever possible.

A variety of terms are used in the literature to describe the negative attitudes associated with computers—computer anxiety, cyberphobia, computerphobia, or technophobia are a few most often used. [T.B.] Jay (1981), one of the first to use the term "computerphobia," provided the following definition: "(a) resistance to talking about computers or even thinking about computers, (b) fear or anxiety toward computers, and (c) hostile or aggressive thoughts about computers."

Although research has established that stress and anxiety reduce an individual's ability to perform effectively ([V.B.] Elder, [E.P.] Gardner, and [S.R.] Ruth, 1987; Torkzadeh and Angulo, 1992), and computer anxiety, in particular, has been found to be predictive of whether technology is used and how technology is used ([C.] Scott and [S.] Rockwell, 1997), Rosen and Well (DeLoughry, 1993) report, "few in higher education and elsewhere in society treat technophobia as a problem worthy of their attention." They say that too many people are under the illusion that computer anxiety will disappear if the world is flooded with technology. Also, Torkzadeh and Angulo (1992) emphasize "computer anxiety is not a transitory problem that will disappear as the current generation of students, who are gaining computer exposure at an early age, move in to the workforce. The computer training and exposure that young people receive in most high schools and colleges is inadequate since the current proliferation of computers will demand more—not less—computer literacy. The increasing demand for strategic use of computer applications will require even more comprehensive and continuous training programmes."

Computer anxiety has implications for instruction and training, both in educational environments and in the workplace explain that organizations need to understand how individual differences relate to computer skill given the growth of end-user computing. As stated by [B.H.] Loyd and [C.] Gressard (1984a), "positive attitudes increase the prospect for achievement in any academic endeavor, and negative attitudes make achievement of competency less likely; empirical study of the relationships among these attitudes will help us clarify the character and significance of computer attitudes among students." [M.M.] Maurer and [Michael R.] Simonson (1993–94) recommend additional research be conducted most specifically to determine personality variables that may relate to computer anxiety. [D.J.] Ayersman (1996) also encourages further study of computer anxiety so that more effective methods can be developed for reducing its detrimental effects.

Given a better understanding of factors that may affect computer attitude, educators and trainers may be able to identify high-risk learners and to introduce appropriate interventions that may help students and end-users improve their attitudes toward computers and realize their full potential in the classroom and on the job. This study was conducted to examine relationships between computer attitude and experience and computer attitude and various personality, demographic, and educational variables. . . .

The Methodology of the Study

The sample consisted of 214 students in six sections of a semester (15 week) computer literacy course at a regional midwestern university. Students enrolled in one of the sections through a process of self-selection during the university registration process during winter 1998 (three sections), summer 1998 (one section), and fall 1998 (two sections). The course satisfied a university liberal studies requirement and was open to all majors. No prerequisites existed and student computer experience ranged from beginner to advanced. Each section met in a regular classroom for 2.5 hours per week and in a computer lab for 1.25 hours per week. . . .

The Purpose of the Study

Despite the technologically-oriented society in which we live, students and employees alike continue to exemplify negative attitudes about using the computer. These attitudes can reduce performance both in the classroom and on the job. Equipped with an understanding of the variables that may affect computer attitudes, educators and trainers could identify these individuals and provide more appropriate learning environments for success to occur. Therefore, the purpose of this study was to investigate the relationship be-tween computer attitudes and computer experience, and se-lected demographic, educational, and personality variables. Based on the Computer Attitude Scale by Loyd and Gres-sard (1984a), three types of computer attitude were studied: (1) computer anxiety, consisting of anxiety toward or fear of computers or learning to use computers; (2) computer con-fidence, relating to confidence in the ability to learn about or use computers; and (3) computer liking, meaning enjoy-ment or liking of computers and using computers.

Studies have proven that experience and training significantly help com-puter users gain more confidence, experience less anxiety, and achieve a more positive attitude.

Hypotheses

Given the lack of conclusive evidence on predictors of computer attitude, a review of the literature suggested con-tinued study of the variables experience, gender, age, per-sonality type, and learning style. Additional demographic and educational factors were also analyzed to determine possible relationships with computer attitude. Based on this analysis of the literature, the following null hypotheses were examined:

1. There is no statistically significant change in computer attitude between the beginning of a computer literacy course and the end of the course.
2. There is no statistically significant relationship between computer experience and initial computer attitude, final computer attitude, or change in attitude.
3. There is no statistically significant relationship between selected demographic/educational variables and initial computer attitude, final attitude, or change in attitude.
4. There is no statistically significant relationship between personality type and initial computer attitude, final computer attitude, or change in attitude.
5. There is no statistically significant relationship between learning style and initial computer attitude, final computer attitude, or change in attitude. . . .

Results: Computer Attitude Change

A simple multiple comparisons test (BonFerroni test) was used to simultaneously determine if the three components of attitude (anxiety, confidence and liking) changed during the semester. The results show that anxiety decreased as the semester progressed. As indicated by the mean decrease of 1.678 between the pre- and post-attitude measures, students reported less anxiety at the end of the course. However, confidence and liking for computers did not significantly change during the semester. Therefore, it can be concluded that Hypothesis 1 is partially rejected. . . .

Results: Relationship Between Attitude Change and Prior Experience

When analyzing the relationship between change in attitude and computer experience, CanCor [Canonical Correlation Analysis] results indicated that only prior courses was marginally significant to attitude on the anxiety subscale with $r=-0.150$ and $p=0.048$. Hypothesis 2 is rejected:
1. Initial computer attitudes:
   a. more prior courses indicated less anxiety and more confidence
   b. more work experience indicated less anxiety, more

confidence, and greater liking

c. ownership indicated less anxiety, more confidence, and greater liking

2. Final computer attitudes:

a. more work experience indicated greater liking

b. ownership indicated less anxiety, more confidence, and greater liking. . . .

Results: Relationship Between Attitude Change and Demographic/Educational Variables

Hypothesis 3, which refers to relationships between demographic/educational variables and initial, final, or change in computer attitudes is rejected as a result of the following results:

1. Initial computer attitudes:

a. lower class status indicated less anxiety, more confidence, and greater liking

b. more credits indicated less anxiety, more confidence, and greater liking

c. older students were more confident and reported greater liking

d. better note-taking skills indicated greater confidence

e. greater interest in the course indicated less anxiety, more confidence, and greater liking

f. more hours spent working on the class indicated more anxiety and less confidence

2. Final computer attitudes:

a. lower class status indicated less anxiety, more confidence, and greater liking

b. older students were less anxious, more confident, and reported greater liking

c. higher GPA indicated more confidence

d. greater interest in the course indicated less anxiety, more confidence, and greater liking

3. Change in computer attitudes:

a. greater interest in the course indicated less anxiety, more confidence, and greater liking

b. more hours spent working on the class indicated less confidence

Results: Relationship Between Attitude Change and Personality Type/Learning Style

The fourth question focused on the relationship between personality type and initial computer attitude, final computer attitude, or change in attitude as measured by the Keirsey Temperament Sorter II. Analysis of variance results failed to reject the hypothesis. No significant relationships on the attitude subscales and personality type were shown for initial attitude. . . .

Analysis of variance procedures were conducted to answer the fifth hypothesis to determine if relationships existed between learning style and initial attitude, post attitude, or change in attitude as measured by the Kolb Learning Style Inventory. Results indicated no significant relationships between initial attitude on any of the subscales and learning style. . . .

Conclusions

The following conclusions are offered based on the findings of this study: (1) anxiety associated with computers may be reduced somewhat through formal classroom instruction; (2) students who have prior computer course experience are more positive about computers at the beginning of an introductory computer course than their peers with less computer-related course experience, but by the conclusion of the semester of instruction, this difference is negligible; (3) students who have work experience using computers have less anxiety, more confidence, and a greater liking of computers at the beginning of a computer course, but this work experience only affects the amount they like to use computers by the conclusion of the course; (4) students who own computers consistently report more positive attitudes toward computers; (5) males and females do not differ in their attitudes toward computers; (6) older students tend to have more positive attitudes toward computers than younger students; and (7) freshmen tend to be more positive about computers than upper classmen.

If computer anxiety can be reduced through a semester of formal computer instruction as was shown in this study, and given the inverse relationship between achievement and anxiety (Elder, Gardner, and Ruth, 1987; Torkzadeh and Angulo, 1992), educators and trainers must continue to emphasize the benefit of formal computer instruction for students and employees. While the present study focused on computer attitudes of university students in a computer literacy experience, these findings may indeed be applicable to training needs in the workplace as well as for the life-long learning essential in our technologically-intensive society. The results suggest that institutions of higher education as well as organizations must provide relevant, structured computer instruction for students and employees.

Given the relationship between work experience and computer attitude, classroom teachers and industry trainers are advised to integrate practical applications into their classroom instruction. Encouraging learners to apply the computer to real world problems provides an important and often overlooked aspect of the educational process. Additionally, given the confirmation that students do experience significant levels of computer anxiety, educators should not ignore its existence. [Tamar] Levine and [Smadar] Donitsa-Schmidt (1998) recommend that teachers periodically evaluate students' attitudes, levels of anxiety, and computer-related self-confidence. Short questionnaires can be administered followed by classroom dialogue to explore the extent and nature of the negativism. Through quantitative as well as qualitative assessment of computer attitudes, teachers can develop a better understanding of their students' attitudes and be able to recommend strategies for coping.

Artificial Intelligence in Medicine

Russ B. Altman

In a presentation to the American Association for Artificial Intelligence, Russ B. Altman outlines in three stages the contributions of artificial intelligence to medicine. Starting in the late 1950s researchers developed a process to aid doctors in diagnosing diseases. During the second stage researchers devised processes to help doctors monitor and treat heavy caseloads of two thousand to twenty-five hundred patients. Altman identifies molecular medicine as the third stage and the focus of twenty-first century medicine; he discusses the status of genome mapping and challenges the profession to develop technology to use biology to serve medicine. Altman is assistant professor of medicine at Stanford University. He is the recipient of a National Science Foundation CARREER Award and is a member of the American College of Physicians and the International Society for Computational Biology.

AI [artificial intelligence] has embraced medical applications from its inception, and some of the earliest work in successful application of AI technology occurred in medical contexts. Medicine in the twenty-first century will be very different from medicine in the late twentieth century. Fortunately, the technical challenges to AI that emerge are similar, and the prospects for success are high.

When I was asked to make this presentation, the organizers specifically asked me to review a bit of the history of AI in medicine (AIM) and to provide an update of sorts. I have therefore taken the liberty of dividing the last 30 years of

Excerpted from "AI in Medicine," by Russ B. Altman, *AI Magazine*, Fall 1999. Copyright © 1999 by the American Association for Artificial Intelligence. Reprinted with permission.

medical AI research into three eras: the era of diagnosis, the era of managed care, and the era of molecular medicine. A description of these eras allows me to review for you some of the early and current work in AIM and then tell you about some of the exciting opportunities now emerging.

Medicine Is an Appropriate Field for Artificial Intelligence

Why is AI in medicine even worth considering? In the late 1950s, medicine was already drawing the attention of computer scientists, principally because it contains so many stereotypical reasoning tasks. At the same time, these tasks are fairly structured and so are amenable to automation. Every medical student learns that when one thinks about a disease, one thinks in an orderly way about epidemiology, pathophysiology, diagnosis, treatment, and then prognosis. These are the bins into which medical information is parsed. These sorts of structured reasoning methods made medicine an attractive application area. In addition, medicine is clearly knowledge intensive, and so at places like Stanford (where knowledge was power), it was very tempting to try to encode knowledge for the purposes of reproducing expert performance at diagnosis and treatment. The working hypothesis was that rich knowledge representations would be sufficient, with only relatively weak inference algorithms required. There was (and is) considerable debate about how complex inference should be for expert performance, but it is clear that medicine is a field in which there is a lot of knowledge required for good performance. It is also clear that physicians constantly feel a sense of overload as they deal with the individual data associated with their patients as well as the content knowledge of medicine that they are trying to apply to the treatment of these patients. I can try to provide a feel for the information-processing load on a physician: A full-time general practitioner is currently expected to longitudinally follow a panel of 2000 to 2500 patients. Of course, the severity of illness varies, but it is clear that physicians need systems (computer or otherwise) to track the data pertaining to these patients and turn it into working hypotheses for diagnosis, treatment, and long-term prognosis.

The other appeal to working in AI in medicine is that the field is large, and so virtually all aspects of intelligent behavior can be studied in one part or another of medicine. You can study issues of image processing, automated management of database information, robotic automation of laboratories, computer-assisted diagnosis, multimedia for physician and patient education, virtual and telesurgery, and many other issues. For some, AI in medicine provides a kinder, gentler, "greener" application area in which to apply their techniques.

Three Eras for AI in Medicine

The first era of AI in medicine was the "Era of Diagnosis." The first aspect of medical reasoning that caught the imagination of AI researchers was the process of collecting clinical data and applying inference rules to make the diagnosis of a disease. This is the common image of the doctor as sleuth, determining what disease is causing the patient's symptoms. The second era of AI in medicine was what I have called the "Era of Managed Care of Chronic Disease." This era has approached a set of problems quite distinct from those tackled in the preceding period, as I will discuss. Finally, we are on the precipice of the "Era of Molecular Medicine," which is once again going to raise issues that are different from those occupying researchers during the first two. . . .

In the late 1960s the National Library of Medicine (NLM) (www.nlm.nih.gov/) was established as one of the National Institutes of Health (NIH). This was remarkable for many reasons, not least of which was that most institutes within the NIH are associated with an organ or a disease (for example, The National Institute of Heart, Lung, and Blood or The National Cancer Institute). The NLM is still in search of its organ or disease. Nevertheless, the extramural research program of the NLM has been a principal source of research funds for AI in medicine. The principal intramural contribution from the NLM was the creation of an online database of the published biomedical literature, MEDLINE. Having gone through a number of transformations, the MEDLINE database was recently made available to the general public via the PUBMED resource on the World Wide Web (www.ncbi.nlm.nih.gov/PubMed/). For better or worse (I believe for the better), physicians and patients now have unprecedented access to a literature that is growing exponentially. The challenges in indexing, searching, and parsing this literature represent a major challenge to AI investigators. . . .

Chronic Disease

So what happened to the Era of Diagnosis? All of these systems were evaluated, and all of them seemed to perform near the level of human experts. Well, there were a few problems. First, physicians did not embrace these technologies. Clinical data, unlike billing data, were not routinely available in a digital form, so when you ran these programs there were these very awkward interfaces that asked you lots of questions in order to get the information necessary to do the diagnosis. Clinicians simply did not want to spend time entering data that were already written into a note using natural language. The AI in medicine community realized that they needed electronic medical records as a prerequisite infrastructural element to allow the deployment of these technologies. Thus, issues of knowledge representation, automatic data acquisition, federation of databases, and standard terminologies became quite important. The second problem for diagnostic programs was that physicians did not want help with diagnosis. Diagnosis is fun, and physicians are trained to do it well in medical school and only improve with years of practice. They did not want to give up that fun to a computer. The most significant problem, however, was that diagnosis is a actually very small part of what physicians do in the delivery of medicine. Most visits to a physician are for an existing, previously diagnosed problem. The challenge to the physician is to follow the problem and respond to its evolution intelligently. Diagnosis is a relatively rare event, probably accounting for less than 5 percent of physician time. What physicians really need is help following chronic and slowly evolving disease in 2500 patients that are seen in brief episodes but require expert interventions. So we have the era of chronic care driving AI in medicine research. This problem is compounded by an aging population with more chronic diseases.

There is one other element of medicine that has changed the imperatives for AI research, and this is the emergence of new economic models for funding medicine. The traditional model has been fee for service: A physician performs a service and gets paid an agreed-upon amount. If the physician performs lots of services, the physician makes more money. The new model of medical funding is based on a standard rate per patient that is paid to a physician, regardless of the usage of services by the patient. Now, the financial incentives are reversed. If the physician provides a service, then its cost in time and resources is taken out of the pot of money that represents potential profit. Now physicians still want to treat illness, but there is now a huge incentive to deliver cost-effective, high-quality care. Systems for supporting these activities become the mandate.

One of the ways to reduce the cost of health care is to move it out of expensive hospital rooms and into outpatient clinics. So instead of intense episodes in the hospital, we have these much more frequent less intense episodes in the clinic where similar things are being done but in a more fragmented manner. The fragmentation may cause confusion as we ask physicians to track the progress of 2500 patients with periodic interactions. . . .

The Era of Molecular Medicine

Although the management of chronic disease under conditions of capitated payment are likely to continue, I believe that there is an even more revolutionary set of changes coming to medicine. These changes will arise from the work being done in basic biology in determining the complete DNA sequence of both the human organism as well as most major disease-causing organisms. There is an excellent paper in the IAAI-98 proceedings by Rick Lathrop and coworkers that is an example of the opportunities in linking molecular concepts with medical care and AI research.

First, it is appropriate to give some background about the genome sequencing efforts. The entire development, structure, and function of an organism is specified by a sequence of four DNA letters: A, T, C, and G are the abbreviations of their chemical names (energy). A human organism is specified by 3 billion letters, arranged serially, that constitute its genome. With 2 bits per DNA letter, it takes about 750 megabytes of data to specify a human. There are 23 chromosomes that divide these 3 billion into subsegments for logistical reasons, with an average length of 256 million DNA letters. Genes are subsequences within the sequence of 3 billion that encode for particular functions or structures that exist in your body. There are about 100,000 genes within a human genome. More than 99.9 percent of the genome is identical for all humans. And so all the diversity of human life is contained in the 0.1 percent that is different. One of the human genes encodes a channel that allows a chloride ion to pass from the outside of a cell to its inside. This channel sometimes has a mutation that leads to the disease cystic fibrosis. An understanding of how the DNA letters differ in patients with cystic fibrosis allows biologists to begin to understand the mechanism of the disease and ways to alter its course. The cystic fibrosis gene was isolated in a relatively expensive, focused manner before the genome sequencing project was under way. The logic behind a genome project is to isolate all genes for an organism and catalog them using economies of scale. The primary genome project is the Human Genome Project, but there are also genome projects for important model organisms and organisms that cause human disease. The principal funding agencies for the genome project are the National Institutes of Health (via the National Human Genome Research Institute, www.nhgri.nih.gov/) and the Department of Energy (www.er.doe.gov/ facepage/hug.htm).

New Technologies Associated with the Genome Will Aid Medicine

Associated with the genome sequencing projects are a number of other new technologies in biology that will allow data to be collected on a large scale, never before possible. Soon it will be possible to assess the complete set of genes that are active in a cell and compare this set with the genes that are active in a diseased version of the same cell. Thus, we can find out which genes are active in a normal prostate cell as well as which genes are active in a prostate cancer cell. The differences are the obvious places to look for new treatments of prostate cancer. The differences may also provide new ways to make a more sensitive and specific diagnosis of prostate cancer in a patient. Finally, the differences may be used to determine the likely prognosis of a particular prostate cancer, based on its constellation of genes, and whether they are associated with an indolent or aggressive type of cancer.

Having defined all the genes in a biological system, there are incredible opportunities for information storage, retrieval, and analysis technologies. First, the epidemiology of disease will now have a molecular basis. We will track the spread of infections by identifying the unique sequences of the offending bacteria and using this as a signature to follow its spread through the population. For example, investigators have tracked the spread of tuberculosis with these technologies. Second, clinical trials will have patients who are stratified by the differences and similarities in their genes. We will be able to relate particular clinical syndromes to particular treatments based on a molecular understanding of the basis of these syndromes. The diagnosis of many diseases will become a simple lookup in the genome of the patient to see which variant is present. We will be able to focus treatments using this information, once we have learned from the data the best drugs to use against different disease/gene variations. Finally, we will have prognostic information beyond anything currently available because we will have access to the full genetic endowment of a patient and, when relevant, the infectious pathogens causing disease. In some cases, in fact, we may know decades before a disease is evident that a patient is at high risk for that disease. At this point, it is important to mention the ethical, social, and legal issues associated with the Human Genome Project. A certain fraction of the annual genome project budget is spent on grants addressing these issues, including issues of privacy, ethical use of medical information, patients' rights to information, and the like (www.nhgri.nih.gov/About_NHGRI/Der/Elsi/).

Genome Data Are Easily Accessible

What's the status of the genome sequencing projects? Although this is not AI per se, it is useful to get a feeling for the amounts and types of data that are being generated. Consider the GENBANK database of DNA sequences. A recent release of that database contained 1.6 billion bases. (Remember, there are 3 billion bases in a human). However, this database contains DNA sequences from all organisms, and not just humans. All these data are available on the World Wide Web, and one of the remarkable aspects of the explosion of biological data is the ease in which it can be accessed, and so it becomes something of a playground for information scientists who need to test ideas and theories. . . . For example, we have roughly 700 million bases of human genome sequence. The human genome is currently scheduled to be completed around 2003. Other organisms include important laboratory test organisms (for example, mouse, rat, or fruit fly) or human pathogens (for example, the HIV virus, malaria, syphilis, or tuberculosis). One of the most exciting challenges that arises as we learn the complete genetic background of bacteria is to develop comparative methods for understanding how differences in genetic endowment create differences in preference for mode of infection, type of infection, and virulence. Table 1 shows some organisms whose genomes are completely known.

Table 1. Some Completed, Fully Sequenced Genomes.

Aquifex aeolicus (bacteria that grows at 85 [degrees] to 95 [degrees] C!)

Archaeoglobus fulgidus (bacteria that metabolizes sulfur, lives at high temperature)

Bacillus subtilis (ubiquitous soil bacteria)

Borrelia burgdorferi (causes Lyme Disease)

Chlamydia trachomatis (causes blindness in developing countries)

Escherichia coli (can cause urinary tract infections, dysentery)

Haemophilus influenzae (causes upper respiratory infections)

Methanobacterium thermoautotrophicum (bacteria that produces methane, lives at 70 [degrees] C)

Helicobacter pylori (causes ulcers, maybe cancer)

Methanococcus jannaschii (bacteria that produces methane)

Mycobacterium tuberculosis (causes tuberculosis)

Mycoplasma genitalium (smallest genome of known independent organisms)

Mycoplasma pneumoniae (causes "walking pneumonia")

Pyrococus horikoshii (grows best at 98 [degrees] C!)

Saccharomyces cerevisiae (baker's yeast)

Treponema pallidum (causes syphillis). . . .

Intelligent agents are being designed to assist biologists in understanding and mining the data that are accumulating from the new high-throughput biological experiments. The National Center for Biotechnology Information (www.ncbi.nlm.nih.gov/) is the clearing house for many sources of useful biological data. Their collection includes data about DNA sequences, human genetic diseases, protein and nucleic acid structures, the biomedical literature, and other important sources. The good news is that this information is easily available. The bad news is that it is not yet integrated in a manner that allows rapid discovery and inferencing. Thus, a biologist with lots of time can eventually find the answer to a question using these databases, but they have not yet been distilled to the point where a physician in a clinical practice can use the data to guide clinical decision making. The intelligent integration of biological information thus becomes one of the major bottlenecks in progress for information processing (Markowitz and Ritter 1995).

Ten Challenges to Medicine

I want to end my presentation with the 10 grand challenges to medicine I have previously proposed. These can be divided into infrastructure, performance, and evaluation goals and are summarized here:

Infrastructure Challenges

1. We need an electronic medical record based on semantically clean knowledge representation techniques.

2. We need automated capture of clinical data, from the speech, natural language, or structured entry, in order to provide the data required to move forward.

3. We need computable representations of the literature. Both clinical and basic biology data should be structured and universally accessible for automated data analysis.

Performance Challenges

4. We still need to do automated diagnosis. Despite the passing of its era, it is still worth understanding because there are times it is useful.

5. We need automated decision support for providers who interact with patients episodically and need help in making decisions about the treatment trajectory.

6. We need systems for improving access to information and explanation for patients.

7. We need systems to provide and document continuing education for physicians.

Evaluation Challenges

8. We need demonstrations of the cost-effectiveness of advanced information technology.

9. We need to create new medical knowledge with machine-learning and/or data-mining techniques. Having established the data infrastructure for clinical data and biological data, there will be unprecedented opportunities for gaining new knowledge.

10. Finally, we need to ensure that there is equitable access to these technologies across patient and provider populations.

Conclusions

The Era of Diagnosis got things rolling and created excitement as existing inferencing strategies were tested in the real-world application domain of medicine. The current Era of Chronic Disease and Managed Care has changed the focus of our efforts. The coming Era of Molecular Medicine contains challenges that can keep information technologists busy for decades.

Virtual Communities Can Strengthen Local Communities

Andrew L. Shapiro

Andrew L. Shapiro acknowledges the advantages and pleasures that individuals derive from virtual communities, but he argues that excessive participation in them is dangerous because participants lose their feelings of loyalty to and cohesion with their local geographic communities. Shapiro suggests a compromise. He recommends community networks or, even better, local gateways that connect people within a community by Internet as well as allow them to surf globally. He identifies guidelines for establishing these local gateways. Shapiro is a *Nation* contributing editor and a fellow at the Brennan Center for Justice at New York University Law School. He is the author of *The Control Revolution*.

The increasing popularity and usage of the Internet has redefined the notion of community, as users are able to communicate and form bonds with people all over the world. Individual users have the power to go where they wish with little or no regulation in the virtual communities.

There is a common thread underlying such developments. It is not just a change in how we compute or communicate. Rather, it is a potentially radical shift in who is in control of information, experience and resources. The Internet is allowing individuals to make decisions that once were made by governments, corporations and the media. To an unprecedented degree, we can decide what news and entertainment we're exposed to and whom we socialize with. We can earn a living in new ways; we can take more control of how goods are distributed; and we can even exercise a new degree of political power. The potential for personal growth and social progress seems limitless. Yet what makes this shift in power—this control revolution—so much more authentic than those revolutions described by techno-utopian futurists is its volatility and lack of preordained outcome.

Contrary to the claims of cyber-romantics, democratic empowerment via technology is not inevitable. Institutional forces are resisting, and will continue to resist, giving up control to individuals. And some people may wield their new power carelessly, denying themselves its benefits and imperiling democratic values. Nowhere are the mixed blessings of the new individual control more evident than in the relationship of the Internet to communities—not just "virtual communities" of dispersed individuals interacting online but real, geographically based communities.

The Internet Offers People the Opportunity to Shape Personal Experiences

The Internet's impact on community has everything to do with a digital phenomenon known as personalization, which is simply the ability to shape one's experience more precisely— whether it's social encounters, news, work or learning. Traditionally, friendships and acquaintances have been structured by physical proximity; we meet people because they are our neighbors, classmates, co-workers or colleagues in some local organization. Much of our information intake— newspapers and radio, for example—also reflects locality, and we share these media experiences and others (like national television) with those who live around us. The global reach and interactivity of the Internet, however, is challenging this. Individuals can spend more time communicating and sharing experiences with others regardless of where they live. As Internet pioneer J.C.R. Licklider wrote back in the sixties, "Life will be happier for the on-line individual because the people with whom one interacts most strongly will be selected more by commonality of interests and goals than by accidents of proximity."

Virtual communities are perfect for hobbyists and others

with quirky or specialized interests—whether they're fans of swing music, chemistry professors or asthma sufferers. Indeed, these associations suggest the possibility of whole new forms of social life and participation. Because individuals are judged online by what they say, virtual communities would appear to soften social barriers erected by age, race, gender and other fixed characteristics. They can be particularly valuable for people who might be reticent about face-to-face social interaction, like gay and lesbian teenagers, political dissidents and the disabled. ("Long live the Internet," one autistic wrote in an online discussion, where "people can see the real me, not just how I interact superficially with other people.")

The Internet also gives individuals a new ability to personalize their news, entertainment and other information. And studies of Internet use show that users are doing so. Rather than having editors and producers choose what they read, hear and watch—as with newspapers or television—they are using the interactivity of the Net to gather just the material they find interesting. This may, among other things, be a winning strategy for dealing with the torrent of information that is increasingly pushed at us.

Extreme Personalization Undermines Local Communities

There is, in fact, plenty to like about personalization. But if we're not careful, customizing our lives to the hilt could undermine the strength and cohesion of local communities, many of which are already woefully weak. For all the uncertainty about what "community" really means and what makes one work, shared experience is an indisputably essential ingredient; without it there can be no chance for mutual understanding, empathy and social cohesion. And this is precisely what personalization threatens to delete. A lack of common information would deprive individuals of a starting point for democratic dialogue, or even fodder for the proverbial water-cooler talk. For many decades, TV and radio have been fairly criticized for drawing us away from direct interaction in our communities. Yet despite this shortcoming (and many others), these mass media at least provide "a kind of social glue, a common cultural reference point in our polyglot, increasingly multicultural society," as media critic David Shaw puts it.

Online experiences rarely provide this glue. Yes, we can share good times with others online who enjoy the same passions as we do. We can educate ourselves and even organize for political change. But ultimately, online associations tend to splinter into narrower and narrower factions. They also don't have the sticking power of physical communities. One important reason for this is the absence of consequences for offensive behavior online; another is the ease of exit for those who are offended. In physical communities, people are inextricably bound by the simple difficulty of picking up and leaving. On the Net, it's always "where do you want to go today?" Are you bored? Ticked off? Then move on! For many, this makes the virtual life an attractive alternative to the hard and often tiresome work of local community building.

Some might think that the weakness of online affiliations would prevent them from posing any real challenge to physical communities. But the ability to meander from one virtual gathering to the next, exploring and changing habitats on a whim, is exactly the problem. The fluidity of these social networks means that we may form weak bonds with others faraway at the expense of strong ties with those who live near us.

Finding a Balance Between Personal Desire and Communal Obligations

Few people, of course, intend to use the Internet in ways that will cause them to be distracted from local commitments. But technology always has unintended consequences, and social science research is beginning to show how this may be true for the Internet. Researchers who conducted one of the first longitudinal studies of the Internet's social impact, the HomeNet study, were surprised when their data suggested that Internet use increases feelings of isolation, loneliness and depression. Contrary to their starting hypotheses, they observed that regular users communicated less with family members, experienced a decline in their contacts with nearby social acquaintances and felt more stress. Although the authors noted the limitations of their findings, the study's methodology has been widely criticized. Until more conclusive results are available, however, what's important is that we take seriously the hazards outlined in the HomeNet study and attempt to prevent them from becoming worse or taking root in the first place.

And how should we do that? Neo-Luddites would likely recommend rejecting technology and returning to our bucolic roots. A more balanced and realistic response, however, calls for a reconciling of personal desire and communal obligations in a digital world. On the one hand, this means acknowledging the sometimes exhilarating adventure of indulging oneself online. No one can deny the value of being able to form relationships with far-flung others based solely on common interests. At the same time, it means not having illusions about the durability of those bonds or their ability to satisfy fully our deepest needs.

We must recognize, for selfish and societal reasons alike, the importance of focusing on the local. This is where we will find a true sense of belonging; shared experience, even if not ideal, creates a sense of commitment. This is where democracy and social justice must first be achieved; getting our own house in order is always the first priority. The Net must therefore be a vehicle not just for occasional escapism but for enhanced local engagement—online and off.

Community Networks Strengthen Local Communities

Efforts to employ technology to strengthen local communities are not new. They have been tried since the dawn of cable television in the seventies and, for more than sixty years, via community radio programming. Those technologies, though, are one-to-many. What makes the Net so promising as a tool of localism is its capacity for interactivity, as well as its nearly unlimited capacity.

Many early Internet enthusiasts have been strong supporters of "community networking," an approach that encourages locally based online communication, often at no charge to users. Community networking has its origins in services such as the Free-Nets, which emerged in the eighties and early nineties to offer online access, sometimes along with local news and information. Most Free-Nets were noncommercial, with no advertising and no subscription charges. Often, they were text-based bulletin board systems run voluntarily by computer enthusiasts. And often they were not easy for novices to use.

A good share of these early services, in addition, were not so much about local affairs as they were a way for residents to get online for free. As a result, Free-Nets and other community networks suffered as America Online and other inexpensive (and more alluring) gateways to the Net became available. By the late nineties, many had gone out of business, as did the National Public Telecommunications Network, an umbrella group of Free-Nets that was founded in 1986. Still, more than a hundred Internet-based community networks in the United States have continued to thrive, such as Charlotte's Web in Charlotte, North Carolina; Liberty Net in Philadelphia; the Seattle Community Network; and Blacksburg Electronic Village in Blacksburg, Virginia.

Arising from a project that began in 1984, Blacksburg Electronic Village appears to be one of the more successful of these endeavors. It counts a majority of Blacksburg's 36,000 residents as participants. Senior citizens chat with their neighbors online. Parents keep abreast of what their kids are doing in school and exchange e-mail with teachers. Citizens use Web-based surveys to communicate with their municipal government about spending priorities. A key feature of successful community networks, in fact, is the opportunity they provide citizens to talk—with civic leaders and one another. Users don't just want information fed to them; they want to generate conversation themselves.

In a community network in Amsterdam, for example, citizens talk about keeping the city's largest park in shape, they argue about Amsterdam's proposed transformation from city to province and they bombard politicians with questions about Holland's abstruse tax laws. Similar results were apparent even in a short-term case study involving a group of

London neighbors. Microsoft gave them computers, Internet access and a way to communicate with one another online. Participants used the technology to exchange information about local services. Kids asked questions about homework. There was a debate about a proposed change in local parking rules, and some members even organized to do something about disruptive vibrations from a nearby railroad. The dialogue, moreover, appeared to translate into stronger ties among neighbors. "I used to know maybe five or six people in the street; now I know at least forty of them quite well, and some very closely," one participant said.

Even some early online services that didn't start as community networks appear to have succeeded precisely because members were located mostly in one geographic area. The Well, a pioneering online community based in San Francisco (and recently bought by Salon, the Internet-magazine-turned-portal), was never intended to be about the Bay Area or just for people from there, yet its founders knew from the start that a sense of local culture would be an important component of the online community. Most interestingly, perhaps, they recognized the value that regular face-to-face contact would have for members. Monthly Well parties were therefore instituted in the San Francisco area and became an important element of the online community's identity. Similarly, Echo, a prominent New York–based online community, offers regular events such as readings, a film series, bar gatherings and softball games. As Echo's mission statement says, "We know that the best online communities are never strictly virtual." Contrary to the utopian notion that the Internet will lift us above the confines of geography, then, the history of online communities suggests that people want to convene with their geographic neighbors, both online and in person.

Local Gateways Should Have Local/Global Balance

Given this fact and the success of some community networks, it might seem that little needs to be done to achieve balance between our desire to surf globally and our need to network locally. Yet as the Internet presents the possibility of a more alluring universe of distractions and greater social isolation, emphasis on localism must become stronger and more explicit. We need to build high-quality, Web-based local networks that are ubiquitous, accessible and interesting enough so that all Internet users will want to use them, at least some of the time. This would insure a degree of involvement with community issues and engagement with actual neighbors. These networks should not be final destinations, though. Instead, reflecting a local/global balance, they should be thought of as local gateways to the global Net—and to offline interaction, as well.

Like entry ramps, these gateways should allow users to go anywhere. Yet, learning from the successes and failures of predecessors, they must provide stimulating content about local issues and an opportunity for users to talk with one another. There should be resources and discussion about issues that people really care about: recreation and entertainment, sports teams, politics, schools, shopping and consumer assistance, and crime and safety. This alone should entice people to visit. And as local gateways facilitate dialogue among community members, eventually empathy, interdependence and cooperative action will follow.

For users without Internet access, the local gateway could be the service they call to get online—for free. (The goals of universal access and localism could therefore be intertwined.) Following the lead of existing community networks, Internet terminals could be put in schools and libraries, churches, public housing projects and recreation centers. For those who already have online access, the local gateway could be used as a portal site on the Web.

Guidelines for Local Gateways

The architecture of the local gateway is crucial. Its blueprint should be influenced not just by a local/global balance but by other democratic values. For example, citizens should be able to speak freely and be heard (even if they can't pay for prominent positioning on the site), privacy should be protected and public-interest resources should be readily available and easy to use. This online "commons" must be a worthy complement to the physical public commons—not a substitute, but an extension. It should thus have all the quirks and flavor of the geographic community for which it is a digital annex, and it should be accountable to the members of that community.

In terms of content and design, there are two models for the kind of local gateway I am proposing. One is existing community networks, which are generally superb examples because they emphasize localism and citizen dialogue. Sometimes, though, community networks are an end in themselves, instead of an entrance to the whole Net. To draw a larger audience, the gateway format is better, because it becomes a routine starting place for users, while not confining them. The opposition by some community networks to partnering with business may also be counterproductive. Blacksburg Electronic Village, for one, claims to have benefited greatly from the fact that it began as a partnership among government (the town of Blacksburg), academia (Virginia Tech, which provided most of the funding) and industry (Bell Atlantic, the local phone company, which recently pulled out after four and a half years). More than two-thirds of local businesses are on the Blacksburg network, which makes it convenient for users. It also gives a boost to local vendors who might otherwise lose substantial business to huge Internet companies based outside the community— a trend that technology critic Richard Sclove aptly calls the "cybernetic Wal-Mart effect."

At the same time, local gateways should not be overly commercialized. In particular, citizens should shun attempts by corporations to fabricate communities just so they can use members as a target audience for sales and advertising. It's a practice that has been tried on the Web, though fortunately with little success so far. Businesses would be better off working in cooperation with community groups and local governments. And citizens should welcome their participation, so long as they have a local presence and maintain a civic-minded spirit. In fact, the cybernetic Wal-Mart effect could be offset, to a degree, by the ability of community members to patronize online versions of their favorite neighborhood stores, thus supporting their community's tax base, employment and conviviality.

An unlikely boost for local gateways might also come from city-oriented commercial Web services such as those provided by CitySearch, Yahoo, Microsoft's Sidewalk and AOL's Digital Cities. Some American cities have as many as a half-dozen of these sites competing for the public's attention. With their collection of local news, weather and services such as free e-mail, these sites provide a second model for local gateways. Community networking activists have traditionally seen them as the enemy because of their commercialism and the fact that they attract individuals away from nonprofit sites. Yet under the right circumstances, these sites could help anchor individuals in their communities. They could become partners in the formation of local gateways. (Austin Free-Net, for example, has worked closely with the for-profit Austin CitySearch.)

Citizens Need to Act

For this to happen, citizens need to leverage the power that interactive technology gives them. We need to organize and tell these city-based portals that to win our attention they must give something back to our communities. They must, for example, donate substantial online resources—such as free Web site hosting and design, chat forums, dial-up access and hardware—to tenant groups, parent-teacher associations, charitable entities, activist groups and other community-based organizations. They must offer Internet authoring tools that anyone can use to create a dialogue forum. And they must find people to lead moderated discussions and otherwise work to strengthen communal conversation. (If city-based portals are unresponsive to citizen action, activists should investigate the possibility of government regulation to achieve at least some of these aims.)

Finally, local gateways should not be seen as a panacea for community activism. They must instead be part of a larger strategy of face-to-face local engagement—which may nonetheless be more effective and more enjoyable thanks to local online interaction, as for example in the London experiment.

Steam and rail gave us the opportunity to flee far from our places of birth; telegraph and telephone allowed us to conduct our business and social lives from a distance; television insulated us further even as it sometimes gave us common experiences. The goal of the Internet revolution, if it can be said to have one, should not be to replicate the world we know, but to improve it. As we explore the farthest reaches of our new World Wide Web, we must also use technology to fortify the local webs in which we dwell.

The Impact of Computers on Daily Life

Douglas S. Robertson

Douglas S. Robertson enumerates ways the computer has made a profound impact on daily life in America within a generation. He explains how unseen 8-bit computer chips are integral to common, useful objects from appliances to watches to photographic equipment. He explains the functions of computers installed in automobiles and security systems and the effects of computers on shopping habits and research. In the future, according to Robertson, hardly anything will be left untouched by computers. Robertson teaches geological sciences at the University of Colorado. He is the author of "The Information Revolution," published in *Communications Research*, and *The New Renaissance: Computers and the Next Land of Civilization*.

Many of the changes wrought by the new computer technology will be nearly invisible to the user. Computers will be embedded in familiar products and appliances, and the consumer will be aware only that these products now have more capabilities, better performance and reliability, and lower cost. The magnitude of the phenomenon of "invisible" computing can be illustrated with one arresting statistic on computer chip production: The dollar value of 8-bit computer chips (such as the Z80) produced and sold in 1996 was on the order of $5.7 billion. In contrast, sales of more advanced 16- and 32-bit chips came to only $1.6 billion.

The reason this number is extraordinary may require a bit of explanation. As I write this in 1997, CPU [central pro-

---

cessing unit] chips have gone through at least five "genera-tions" from the 8-bit Z80 to the 16-bit 80286 to the 32-bit 80386, 80486, Pentium, and beyond. Indeed, the 8-bit chips are so obsolete that some 8-bit computer systems are already behind glass in museum displays. Yet 8-bit chips are still being produced in record numbers. There are three basic reasons for this: First, the 8-bit chips have computer power comparable to a mainframe computer of the early 1960s; second, the chips can be produced for less than a dollar each; and third, there is a huge demand for them. None of this vast volume of 8-bit chip production is going into conven-tional personal computers as it did a decade ago. Today all of it is going into appliances, microwave ovens, televisions, telephones, dishwashers, videotape recorders, and other products where the users are seldom aware that they are op-erating a sophisticated computer. The users know only that the capabilities of these appliances have multiplied with lit-tle change in their overall price.

Perhaps the most familiar symbol of invisible computer power is found in the humble wristwatch. A generation ago the finest wristwatches were mechanical marvels containing intricate machinery of miniaturized springs and gears that were crafted with jewel-like precision. In contrast, today's wristwatch has almost no moving parts. I am presently wear-ing a watch that has a quartz oscillator accurate to a few sec-onds per month. The watch has a calendar display that not only knows the days of the week and the duration of each month but is programmed to handle and display leap-year dates correctly until the year 2100 (the next four-year span that lacks a leap year). It also has an alarm buzzer that can be set for a particular time of day and for a particular day of the year. It has a stopwatch and a count-down mode and a dual-time mode (for keeping track of two time zones) and twelve-or twenty-four-hour display. All of this technology is avail-able at a cost of about $25. Nothing remotely comparable was available in watches costing a hundred times as much as recently as a generation ago.

Another dramatic impact of computer technology will be found in personal transportation, particularly in the operation of automobiles. It has often been remarked that the average automobile today has more on-board computer power than the Apollo moon lander. Most of this technology is presently used to adjust and refine engine performance, and it is therefore in the "invisible-to-the-user" category. But new computer technology is being developed that will have much more visibility to the operator or driver. [Writing in *PC Magazine*, B.] Howard (1997) recently described Global Positioning System (GPS) satellite-positioning technology that can be coupled with computer displays to show the current position of a vehicle on a computer-displayed map. This technology is already available and will become universal as its cost plummets. This navigational software can be programmed to give piloting instructions, by voice if desired ("Turn left at the next intersection." "You missed the turn at the last intersection. Should I recalculate the best route from this point?").

Fully automated automobile operation (driving) is almost possible with this technology, except for some minor details such as collision avoidance. And computerized technologies are being developed to handle collision avoidance as well through the use of radar, sonar, and optical sensing techniques. Such technology is already available for aircraft, and one freeway in California is already being outfitted with instruments as a test site for automatic automobile piloting. The technology will have to be made nearly fail-safe, or at least it will have to represent a substantial improvement over ordinary human operation of the automobile, but this should not be a difficult standard to achieve.

Computers in Business and Communication

The popularity of personal finance, checkbook balancing, and tax preparation software indicates another broad area in which computers can have an impact on our personal lives. All of us have a substantial need for the tedious and extensive arithmetic operations involved in the calculation of tax payments, planning of estates, and general financial decision making. In the past there were only two options for doing this kind of work: You could hire expensive professionals to do the work for you, or you could attempt the detailed calculations yourself, slowly, tediously, and frequently with errors. Today, computer software is available that can simplify and streamline these tasks and bring fast, accurate, and inexpensive results within everyone's reach. Even minor legal matters such as writing wills and filing routine court papers can be handled by the appropriate software. . . .

Another area being revolutionized by computer technology is personal communication. Cellular phone technology has changed the way we think about telephone service. This technology has led to unexpected adventures such as the case of the party of hikers in the San Juan Mountains in Colorado, one of whom fell and suffered serious injuries at a point that was many hours of hiking distance from the nearest road. Instead of hiking out, one of the other members of the party retrieved a cellular phone from his backpack, dialed 911, and telephoned out the GPS satellite coordinates of the party to a rescue crew. A helicopter evacuated the injured man within the hour. . . .

Computers Affect Our Comfort and Security

The use of electronic technology for photography, both still and video, is growing explosively. This technology allows us to do more than record our vacations and our children at play. It may have a deep impact on law enforcement, for example, as the Rodney King case in Los Angeles illustrates. And a recent advertisement for an electronic still camera contained an unconscious irony: The advertisement touted the camera's use for police work in documenting evidence and crime scenes, and then described how a realtor could use it to photograph a property for sale and then digitally alter the image to remove unsightly trash cans. The incompatibility of the two uses was apparently lost on the advertising writer.

Computers have already had more impact on the operation of our homes than many of us are aware of, thanks to invisible computers. The simple thermostat on the wall of my own house, for example, is no longer the humble bimetal strip of years past, but rather is a sophisticated computer connected to several digital thermometers. The computerized thermostat is programmed to adjust not just the temperature of the house but the rate of change of temperature in order to achieve optimum performance of the furnace/air conditioner system at varying times of the day and week. Whereas earlier models of timed thermostats merely changed the temperature setting at a given time, this thermostat holds a target time at which the new temperature setting is to be achieved. It then checks to see if the desired time is actually met, and adjusts itself when the target is missed.

Computerized home security devices are already available. These devices can alert the police or fire department if an intruder or fire is detected. Motion sensor technology can be used to turn on lights outside the front door if someone approaches. Future advances in home security may include such things as door locks operated by fingerprint or retinal pattern recognition. . . .

Computers Make Business and Industry More Efficient

Another modest impact of computer technology is found at the grocery store check-out counter. The barcode scanners provide fast, efficient, and accurate checkout, and operating them requires less training than operating conventional cash registers. There is some concern about the accuracy of the programmed prices, but even this is something of an advantage over old methods of grocery check-out because the errors in the programmed prices can be checked much more easily than random clerical errors. And by creating a computerized record of each transaction, the computerized software can make the process of inventory management and restocking much simpler and less labor-intensive.

But the overall impact of computer technology on marketing and retailing will extend well beyond supermarket check-out lines, of course. For the first time, this past Christmas I did some of my own holiday shopping using the Internet to find products, compare prices and features, and place orders. The ability of computer networks to provide product information and order/sales information could revolutionize marketing. However, if cable TV shopping channels are a sample of the directions in which this technology will develop, then perhaps the less said the better. . . .

Improving the efficiency of industry should have ripple effects throughout the entire economy. To take just one important example, the recent development of just-in-time inventory management for manufacturing has reduced the reliance on costly and inefficient inventory stocks. These techniques have the potential to ameliorate or even eliminate the classic "business cycle" of boom and bust, because those cycles were driven in some measure by excessive build-up of inventories during the "boom" portion of the cycle. If business cycles are indeed eliminated or even just reduced, the effects will be felt personally by a large fraction of the population. None of us (except perhaps economists and opposition politicians) will miss the recurrent cycles of recession and depression.

Another area that has long been touted as ripe for revolution by computer and communication technology is the publishing industry. Some newspapers and journals are already distributed electronically rather than on paper. As this technology becomes widespread these industries will become far more efficient, distributing information that is more up-to-date and, as a side bonus, becoming more environmentally friendly through a vast reduction in the use of paper. Already the use of e-mail is reducing paper usage while at the same time providing faster and more convenient communication than is possible with conventional postal services.

From the Handicapped to the Internet

Yet another area that will have a broad and enormously beneficial impact on many lives involves computer aids for the handicapped. Voice recognition and speech generation technology can be of enormous benefit to the blind as well as to the illiterate, and e-mail opens many of the capabilities of telephone communication to the deaf. Quadriplegics can use detectors based on eye and mouth movements for communication. And the GPS technology described for navigating automobiles has already been adapted for use by the blind, allowing them to navigate easily and unaided to unfamiliar locations. Such aids for the handicapped may not affect many of us, but for those who are benefited the effects are of incalculable value.

Even our system of government is being changed in countless ways by computer technology, with effects ranging from computerized vote tallying to sophisticated polling techniques and targeted political advertising and fund raising. The effects are not wholly bad: The impact of fax technology and e-mail on political matters such as the Tiananmen Square protests in Beijing has been widely reported and discussed. These technologies pose both promises and dangers that will have to be dealt with in the next level of civilization.

The impact of the Internet is perhaps the most dramatic example of the ways that computer technology is transforming everyday life. "Surfing the Web" has transformed the way many of us conduct large portions of our lives, from job searching to socializing to researching important or trivial decisions. It has put vast volumes of information at our fingertips and in our homes: Without leaving my house I can search the catalogs of several nearby libraries, scan airline schedules and order tickets, check weather forecasts across the country, keep tabs on various political organizations and government agencies, and pick up information that I hadn't even guessed was in existence. The ability to "click" on keywords of Web pages opens up networks of information that can take us in completely unexpected directions.

Computers Affect Daily Life with a "Tidal Wave"

Michael Dertouzos of MIT's Laboratory for Computer Science has a new book that itemizes in considerable detail many of the ways we can expect the information revolution to affect our daily lives (1997). The principal focus of his book is on information networks such as the Internet. Dertouzos describes a number of novel concepts including such things as "reverse advertising," the electronic equivalent of newspaper "want ads." With reverse advertising, a prospective buyer would post in an electronic marketplace a precise description of the article that he or she wishes to buy. Potential vendors would scan the marketplace and make bids.

As Dertouzos notes, such a system could be advantageous to both buyers and sellers. And it could be extended so that vendors sell not just existing stock, but would actually manufacture the requested product to order. Such customized mass production or "mass individualized production" is feasible only with the enormous information-processing capabilities of computer networks. Other novel applications of computer networking (among the many described by Dertouzos) include such things as virtual neighborhoods, automatic house doctors, and interactive art. Dertouzos is able to encapsulate the impact of the entire computer revolution through the use of an apt metaphor:

> Information technology would alter how we work and play, but more important, it would revise deeper aspects of our lives and of humanity: how we receive health care, how children learn, how the elderly remain connected to society, how governments conduct their affairs. . . . Most people had no idea that there was a tidal wave rushing toward them.

An effective way to cultivate our understanding of the breadth of the impact of computer technology on our everyday lives today is try to think of activities, either our own or those of our neighbors, friends, and coworkers, that are *not* radically altered by computer technology either presently or in the foreseeable future. The list grows shorter by the year. At one time it seemed to me that mundane housekeeping tasks such as cleaning bathrooms might be immune to this revolution. Not so. Robotic self-cleaning bathroom technology has already been developed and will become widely available as the costs drop. The capabilities for robotic cleaning services vastly extend the areas that are impacted by computer technology. I am hard put today to come up with anything at all that is not already affected in some way, or has no potential to be affected by computer technology. The present impact of the computer revolution is already vast beyond our imagination. And this revolution has been going on for less than a generation.

Pornography and the Internet

Paul J. Becker

Within the range of Internet crimes against children, Paul J. Becker reports primarily on the issue of pornography. In 1997 all but six states had laws prohibiting the possession of child pornography in general. In 1999 twenty-seven states had laws against the involvement of the Internet in child pornography. Recently states have increased the severity of punishment for pornography violations, but prosecuting "virtual" child pornography has proven difficult, according to Becker, who urges better enforcement of all pornography laws. Becker teaches criminology at Morehead State University in Morehead, Kentucky.

States must pass laws empowering officials to find and prosecute those who use technology to exploit children.

One of the ongoing challenges facing state officials is how to keep up with changing technology, especially when that technology is used to commit crimes. Recent news stories have pointed to several cases in which people used the Internet to exploit children.

In February 2001 a man was arrested for kidnapping and sexual assault after he used the Internet to lure a 15-year-old Florida girl to Greece, according to a report by the Associated Press. A 2000 article in the *Columbus Dispatch* recounted online crimes in Ohio, including one in which a junior high school teacher used his computer to engage in "pillow talk" with several students, and another in which a man flew to Houston to have sex with a 13-year-old boy he met online. In 1998 the Portland *Herald-Dispatch* of Maine reported that a convicted child molester had photographed the sexual assault of teen-agers and then posted the images on the Internet.

Excerpted from "The Dark Side of the Internet," by Paul J. Becker, *State Government News*, April 2001. Copyright © 2001 by the Council of State Governments. Reprinted with permission.

These are only a few examples of people who have used technology to sexually exploit children. Even though computers provide the means to exploit children in different ways, this article will focus on one type of exploitation—child pornography.

Child Pornography Laws

While children were being sexually exploited well before the invention of computers or the Internet, this new technology helps provide more opportunities for child pornographers. However, state and federal governments began to address this issue only recently. The federal government did not pass a law prohibiting the distribution of child pornography until the 1970s, and the Supreme Court did not uphold the constitutionality of state laws prohibiting the possession of child pornography until its 1990 ruling *Osborne vs. Ohio*. As recently as 1997, six states (Hawaii, Massachusetts, Mississippi, New Mexico, Vermont and Wyoming) did not have laws prohibiting the possession of child pornography, according to the Office of Juvenile Justice and Delinquency Prevention.

New Mexico passed legislation this year making it illegal to possess child pornography. The 2001 law covers any obscene visual or print medium, with felony punishment of 18 months in prison. While the state already had laws against the manufacture and distribution of child pornography and the sexual exploitation of children, the ban on possession became a political imperative this session. Former speaker of the House Raymond Sanchez, a Democrat, blamed his November election loss on his Republican opponent wrongly portraying him as hindering legislation against child pornography.

Meanwhile, outside the United States, the Canadian Supreme Court only this year upheld the constitutionality of its law prohibiting the possession of child pornography, after two lower courts had ruled it violated that country's right to free expression.

Because laws against child pornography are still fairly new, the penalties outlined in some states may seem light. To address this problem, several states have passed laws making possession of child pornography a felony crime rather than a misdemeanor. In New York, legislation introduced in 1996 by Sen. Owen Johnson made possession of child pornography a class E felony, punishable by up to four years in prison.

In Alaska, legislation sponsored by Sen. Drue Pearce in 1998 increased the penalties for possession of child pornography from a class A misdemeanor, punishable by up to one year in prison, to a class C felony, punishable by up to 10 years in prison. And this year in Missouri, Sen. Chuck Gross introduced a bill to increase the punishment for possession of child pornography from a misdemeanor to a felony. While most states now have laws against the possession of child pornography, many states may need to revisit these statutes to consider the penalties for breaking them.

Does Virtual Pornography Cause Harm or Restrict Free Speech?

In "Courting Unsafe Speech," Wendy Kaminer lays out the arguments for and against criminalizing the distribution of virtual child pornography. She recommends that authorities focus on the production of pornography involving real children rather than on the distribution of depictions of imaginary children.

It is possible, of course, that computer-simulated images of virtual children having virtual sex may encourage pedophiles to act on their impulses or may assist them in seducing children. There is, however, little or no empirical evidence that these images have such dire effects. Congress criminalized virtual child porn anyway.

The Child Pornography Prevention Act of 1996 (CPPA) prohibits computer images that "appear" to show actual children engaged in sex; it also bans advertising, promoting, or describing any sexually explicit images "in such a manner that conveys the impression" that actual children are depicted. Anti-porn activists insist that this ban on virtual porn is essential to protecting children and enforcing laws against actual child pornography, since prosecutors may not be able to distinguish the

The Internet Threat

With the expansion of the number of Web pages, Usenet groups and chat rooms, collectors and distributors of child pornography now have more opportunities than ever to exploit children. Thus, states need to update their laws against child pornography to reflect this new technology. Massachusetts learned this lesson in February when a Superior Court ruled that because the 1977 state law against distributing child pornography does not mention computers, it is not a crime to disseminate child pornography over the Internet.

According to a report by the National Center for Prosecution of Child Abuse, by 1999 only 27 states had laws against child pornography involving a computer, and only six states had laws against using a computer to solicit sex

actual from the virtual variety. Free-speech advocates charge that the CPPA allows for the prosecution of thought crimes, by criminalizing non-obscene renderings of imaginary children engaged in imaginary sex. The federal courts are divided on the constitutionality of this statute: It was struck down by the Ninth Circuit Court of Appeals and upheld by the First, Fourth, and 11th Circuit Courts. The issue is now before the Supreme Court.

Many civil libertarians have long accepted (and supported) bans on depicting actual children engaged in actual sex. Traditional child-porn laws need not rely on speculation about the harm caused by the distribution of sexually explicit images involving minors; they can rely instead on the harm caused by the production of sexually explicit images involving minors.

But laws against depictions of imaginary children can rely only on imaginary evidence of harm. As the Ninth Circuit recently observed in *Free Speech Coalition v. Reno*: "Factual studies that establish the link between computer-generated child pornography and the subsequent sexual abuse of children apparently do not yet exist."

Wendy Kaminer, "Courting Unsafe Speech," *American Prospect*, vol. 12, no. 11, (June 18, 2001), p. 31.

from children. Florida Sen. Steve Geller has introduced a bill (SB 144) that would make it a crime not only for someone in Florida to distribute child pornography over the Internet, but also would give his state jurisdiction if child pornography was sent online to someone in Florida from out of state. Geller compared the transmission of child pornography from out of state to someone standing in Georgia and firing a gun at someone in Florida, arguing that even though the shooter did not enter the state, Florida still would have jurisdiction over the crime.

Geller's bill would also prohibit the solicitation of children for sex over the Internet, and it would protect people who reasonably believe they have viewed child pornography, whether over the Internet or while developing photos, if they report their findings to authorities. A similar bill introduced by Geller in 2000 died because it required people to report child pornography rather than simply protecting those who do from civil lawsuits.

Virtual Victims

One of the most pressing issues facing state officials today is "virtual" child pornography, or images that have been digitally altered to represent exploited children. Because a real child may not have been used to create the image, or a nonpornographic image of a child may have been morphed to create something obscene, this activity can be very difficult to prosecute. In December 1999, the Ninth Circuit Court of Appeals, which covers the Western part of the country, ruled in *Free Speech Coalition vs. Reno* that the section of the Child Pornography and Prevention Act of 1996 prohibiting virtual pornography was invalid. The case has been appealed to the U.S. Supreme Court, which is expected to rule on it sometime this year.

Meanwhile, Vermont and Missouri have passed laws prohibiting virtual pornography, and Arizona and New Mexico have recently taken up similar legislation. Without a law prohibiting virtual pornography, prosecutors must prove that a real victim exists when a defendant argues that the images were generated by a computer. This requirement stymied prosecutors in Virginia, who last year were forced to grant a defendant in a virtual pornography case a plea bargain on five counts of a 91-count indictment because they could not prove a real victim was involved.

Better Enforcement

With new technologies also comes the need for advanced efforts from law enforcement. For example, in Virginia, Attorney General Mark Earley created a Computer Crimes Strike Force in 1999. "Our office is vigorously pursuing purveyors of these images and proposing state legislation to facilitate swift prosecution," he said. "These criminals cannot be allowed to hide behind the supposed anonymity they believe the Internet offers."

Besides prosecuting the distribution of child pornography over the Internet, the force will also investigate consumer fraud conducted in cyberspace, enforce laws banning junk e-mail and track regional and national trends in computer crime. Michigan also recently created an Internet Crime Unit, which operates out of the state attorney general's office. Prior to this, Michigan's Wayne County created an Internet Crime Task Force in 1998, which made 26 arrests in its first two years, 24 of them for sex crimes involving children.

A combination of new legislation that takes into account computer technology and special training for law enforcement appears to be an important first step in dealing with the new challenge of child pornography on the Internet.

Chapter 4

The Technology of the Future

Turning | Points
IN WORLD HISTORY

Finding a Job in the Future

David Siegel

David Siegel predicts the impact of technology on job searching in the future by comparing the typical procedures in 1990 and 2000, and then making projections for 2010. Finding a job in 1990 took months, since the process depended heavily on clerical tasks and sending and transferring paper. By 2000 much of the work of job seekers and employers was done on websites in shorter time. Siegel predicts that by 2010 a universal résumé complete with digital video will reduce the task of finding a job to three working days and a total cost to employers of less than four hundred dollars. Siegel, an Internet strategist, is chairman of a web-design and strategy firm. He is the author of *Creating Killer Web Sites* and *Secrets of Successful Web Sites*.

We ease our way into the year 2010 by following Brad, a senior research scientist at a large biotechnology firm. Brad is ready to move on to a company where he can be more of a key player, and he's prepared to move anywhere in the country for the right opportunity.

Before we see how Brad pursues his next opportunity, let's go back to the start of his career and see how he found his first job. Two decades ago, Brad went to work for a fictional company called Big Biotech Inc. (BBI). Here's how the process worked then.

The 1990 Procedure

July 1990. The research manager at BBI needs another programmer in a hurry. She's been through the process many times before and knows it may take months to fill the position.

Excerpted from *Futurize Your Enterprise: Business Strategy in the Age of E-Customer*, by David Siegel (New York: John Wiley & Sons, 1999). Copyright © 1999 by David Siegel. Reprinted by permission of John Wiley & Sons, Inc.

Sighing, she begins to fill out the four-page job request form.

The job request goes to the division vice president for approval and then moves on to human resources. A clerical worker in HR types the information into a database. A professional copywriter writes the ad, and a buyer places it in different labor-market publications. Two to three weeks after the initial job request, the ad appears in Brad's local paper.

Brad, who's just gotten out of graduate school, has worked with a designer friend to create a nice-looking résumé. They chose a traditional, easy-to-read type style, worked on the layout, and followed the insider's rule for résumé page counts (one page for the résumé, one additional page for each Nobel Prize). Because he's sending his résumé to so many different kinds of companies, Brad's stated objective is fairly generic.

Brad chooses nice-looking paper and envelopes and has the local print shop run out 100 copies on a high-resolution printer. He then spends the entire weekend writing cover letters, printing mailing labels, and licking envelope flaps. The next day, Brad takes the stack of envelopes to the post office and dutifully writes out a check for the postage. One of the letters is addressed to BBI, in response to job #4476, which he's written on the envelope as well as the cover letter. He drops the letters in the mailbox and goes home to wait.

Ten days later, BBI's human resource department puts some 2,000 résumés, including Brad's, into a pouch and sends them to Guam. In Guam, a data-entry company scans the résumés and then edits them, translating the information to the proper format for BBI's database. Per BBI's instructions, all multipage résumés that don't list Nobel Prizes go into the trash. BBI has provided the data-entry company with a standardized form containing a number of fields: last name, first name, address, area of expertise (chosen from a predefined list), job title history, skills, and so on.

Because the information must be in a standard format so that applicants can be matched to job requisitions, many of the résumés require extensive editing. The data-entry company has more than 200 clients in the United States, and each client has its own set of standards. The clients' keywords are similar but not identical, so the company has to be careful not to mix them up.

When all the résumés have been edited and entered in BBI's format, the company in Guam makes a computer tape of the résumé information, sends it by courier to BBI's HR department, and then archives the paper résumés in case the biotech company calls with any questions.

At BBI, the HR staff mounts the tapes and puts the records into the database. Six weeks after getting the research director's job request, the HR department matches job seekers to the job and sends any candidates to the department administrator by intra-office mail.

When the administrator calls the applicants to verify they're still in the job market, he discovers that a tenth of the phone numbers were transcribed incorrectly by the data-entry company (the administrator is supposed to fax those back to Guam for correction, but that rarely happens). A full 50 percent of the applicants have already taken jobs elsewhere. The administrator screens the remaining candidates and hands the résumés of those who make the cut to the hiring manager. It's then a matter of scheduling interviews, identifying the most suitable candidate, and following up with an offer. Because all large companies are this slow at hiring employees, Brad is still in the market for a job. At least six weeks have passed by the time Brad meets with the research manager, who eventually gives him his first job.

The 2000 Procedure

April 2000. After ten years at BBI, Brad is ready for a new challenge. He knows the Web has changed the way people apply for jobs, and he is excited to use the power of the Internet to find his dream job as a research manager.

In 2000, the human resources field is much more technologically sophisticated. There's no need for the résumé designer or the data-entry company in Guam. Company copywriters still write copy, but now the ads appear on the company's web site as well as in the Help Wanted section of the newspaper. To apply for a particular job, Brad fills out an online form. Employers still have to deal with a few paper résumés every week, but 90 percent of the job applications now come in through the Web.

In an electronic version of the company mail room, traffic handlers tag the e-résumé with keywords that help match each résumé to possible jobs within the company. In companies with more advanced computer systems, résumés are routed via e-mail; others must print out the résumés and send them by intra-office mail. Using the power of the World Wide Web, the company has cut the time to interview a new prospect from six weeks to three.

Brad finds himself going from one company web site to the next, checking the job postings and filling out application forms. Every company has a different form. Brad fills out forms for the top ten companies he's interested in. Now he's ready to submit his résumé to the online career centers.

In the year 2000, online career centers are booming. Hundreds of career sites are on the Web, and each promises to expose a job seeker like Brad to thousands of employers (including, possibly, his current one). He can respond to a specific job posting or submit his résumé to the career center's database, which employers periodically mine for prospects.

During Brad's job search, his résumé is duplicated more than 400 times by the online career centers he signed on with. Several biotech companies interview him, and he's eventually offered a management position at Huge Biotech, Inc., that pays quite a bit more than he makes at BBI. He accepts the job but soon discovers that the online centers that spread his résumé so effectively have a drawback he didn't foresee: He's still getting calls from companies who think

---

An Online Standard for Résumés

In 1999, a committee of technical people and human resource managers volunteered to work with a company called Structured Methods (Structured methods.com) to develop a standard markup language for online résumés. They defined the Human Resource Management Markup Language (HRMML), which I expand in this chapter to the concept of Universal Résumé.

Job Availability

One of the fields in The Universal Résumé reflects the intensity of Brad's job search. Volunteers in the HRMML community have now agreed on seven levels of availability:

0. Not available, and not looking.
1. Not looking, but would like to keep tabs on the job market.
2. Willing to be taken to lunch.
3. Willing to take a recruiter's call.
4. Available to interview immediately.
5. Will consider contract work.
6. Looking for temporary work, contract work, or any available position.

he's still in the job market. He sends e-mail messages to all the centers asking that his résumé be removed, but the calls keep coming.

The 2010 Procedure

September 2010. Brad is now a senior scientist at HBI, determined to be the research director at a biotech company. This time his job search is a dramatically different experience.

The key to Brad's newfound control over the job search process is a software standard called the Universal Résumé. It sits on a server, available for free to anyone who wants to use it. The Universal Résumé consists of a series of modules for identity, education, experience, awards, goals, and other relevant personal data. It's actually more like a big software program than a document. No one needs more than five percent of the available fields, as many modules are used only by specific job seekers in specific countries.

Brad can narrow his search to specific kinds of jobs or employers. He can easily tailor his résumé to a start-up or to a larger company by filling out the appropriate modules. With the help of an online wizard, Brad takes only a few minutes to complete his own Universal Résumé.

Brad could drop off his Universal Résumé at different career centers or send it electronically to companies himself, but in 2010, most of the career centers are gone. Instead, Brad simply puts his Universal Résumé on his personal website and waits for companies to come to him.

Now that Brad has decided to leave HBI, he checks Number 4 in the job availability box and goes to bed. By the next morning, dozens of companies' software agents scanning the Web have already noticed his résumé.

In 2010, the VP of research at Giant Biotech, Inc., simply answers a few questions at a search engine, and all the résumés of available people who meet her criteria show up on her screen. She can have Brad on the phone a minute after she decides she needs a new research director. And she can program her Internet software agents to alert her when highly desirable people change their status to "willing to be taken to lunch."

Brad gets a call the next day. No posting of job descriptions. No HR department. No employment databases to manage. The Web has become the database, kept up-to-date by the applicants themselves. Companies don't wait for applicants to knock on their doors. And when the research VP looks at Brad's Universal Résumé, she knows she's looking at the current version and that the information is accurate—no more wrong numbers or out-of-the-market applicants.

If Brad accepts a job offer with Giant Biotech, he'll change his availability field back to zero. Immediately, bots [programs that visit a website] and programs can tell he's off the job market. If Brad is on a short list for a job at another company, a bot will remove him from that list within an hour. The average time it takes to hire a new person is now eight working days. But Brad isn't through using the Web to win his dream job yet.

A Digital Video

In 2010, a new kind of career center—I'll call it Universal Recruiting—provides job seekers like Brad the opportunity to add a digital video introduction to their Universal Résumés. The Universal Recruiting office in Brad's city coaches him and then records a series of live segments: a short introduction that summarizes Brad's goals, a longer introduction that summarizes his schooling and work history, and a segment of his responses to a series of general interview questions. Brad adds his own questions to the interview as well. In the online interview, he is candid in discussing his professional needs and wants, his past successes, and his past weaknesses and how he's addressed them. He also attaches the profile results of his Myers-Briggs personality test. All these become part of his Universal Résumé.

The staff at Universal Recruiting works for Brad. He's willing to pay for their help because he knows that by providing a video interview for employers, he'll be considered for more jobs and more competitive salary packages. The people at Universal Recruiting know that, too, and may allow Brad to defer some of his payment until he gets his new job.

Companies now publish Universal Job Requests on their web sites, so Brad can ask his electronic agent to search for specific jobs online. When he clicks on a job description, he also finds a list of interview questions. He can type in his answers and submit them, along with a pointer to his Universal Résumé, or he can answer the questions on digital video and put it on his personal web site with the other interview videos. The ready access and the quantity and quality of the information Brad has provided make it easy for a hiring manager to determine whether he's worth considering seriously.

Two can play these video games. Companies want to attract not only the best people but also those who would mesh best with the company. If a hiring manager has put a digital video about her business unit and her staff on the company's web site, prospective employees can evaluate the company and the manager they'd be working for to see if they would be a good fit.

Adding video to the hiring process also provides companies with access to people who would be hard to bring in for a personal interview. And the employers and job candidates can make their respective videos at their own convenience and use them again and again. The Universal Interview not only saves the employer and the job seeker time and money, it gives them both more choices—a win for everyone.

Brad's Universal Résumé has two levels of privacy, and he could set up more if he saw the need. The top level is public—doesn't reveal Brad's name or personal information. If a company expresses interest in the work experience and knowledge outlined in the top level, Brad can screen the company and, if he's interested, provide access to the second level. Codes can be designated for specific visitors and uses, and Brad can cancel them anytime he chooses. Eventually, Brad will trust the Universal Recruiting bots to give permission to employers that meet his criteria.

The Résumé on the Web

Brad's Universal Résumé is ready to go. Managers can search for appropriate job candidates, narrow their search lists, request further information from Brad, watch and exchange video interviews online, even e-mail Brad's references—all within 24 hours. With the help of some inexpensive software agents, the Universal Résumé and Universal Recruiting have reduced the time and cost of filling a job opening to around three working days and under $400.

Brad's Universal Résumé is a living document. It resides on his personal web site and is easy to update according to his availability. He can remake his video interviews and his references as often as he likes, but once every five years should be fine. Brad is happy to invest in his Universal Résumé because he knows how well it represents him on the Web. It gives him the responsibility—and the power—to market himself.

Technologies Driving Future Business and Personal Changes

Jason P. McKay

Jason P. McKay identifies five technologies that are driving changes in business and personal life. First, he predicts that broadband technologies—cable and DSL (Digital Subscriber Line)—will deliver voice, video, and Internet on one line. Second, wireless devices will deliver millions more bits per second to provide games, videoconferencing, and synchronized data on handsets. Third, packaged software will be a thing of the past because it will be rented on a temporary basis. Fourth, vendors will provide digital cash, an Internet payment system, to make Internet banking safer and easier. And, fifth, wireless Internet appliances in the home will allow users to insert new products efficiently and easily. McKay is a regular contributor to *Black Enterprise* and TELE.com.

The road to the 21st century has brought many changes in the way we work, conduct our private lives, and do business. And the Internet is at the center of it all. That claim isn't meant to steal any thunder from other advances, but the Internet has changed not only how we communicate but also when, where, and how often.

Other technologies are also heralding a new era. Distance is virtually eliminated with high-speed digital connections; electronic commerce is helping small businesses compete with large corporations worldwide. Wireless devices are no longer luxuries but necessities in a fast-moving marketplace. And biology is slowly but seamlessly meshing with technology. Computing systems that once occupied entire rooms now fit in the palms of our hands.

With so many changes occurring, it's easy to get over-whelmed. To help you keep pace, we've looked at five tech-nologies that are driving change in business and in everyday life.

Broadband

Many of today's homes are crawling along, whether they know it or not, in what will be deemed the dark ages once broadband technologies—cable and DSL—get up to speed. Currently [in 2001], 56Kbps is the fastest modem speed available, although the actual transmission rate tops off at about 52Kbps (or lower, depending on your ISP).

Most homes and smaller businesses with Web access use dial-up because it is the cheapest and most widely available, but DSL and cable providers are making inroads. Broad-band, according to the Federal Communications Commis-sion, is capable of supporting both downstream and up-stream connections at speeds in excess of 7Mbps; that's about four times faster than dial-up. Many small to medium-size businesses already have broadband access, as do con-sumers who want instant-on access, faster surfing, or a bet-ter gaming experience.

And as products and delivery mechanisms evolve, the ca-pabilities broadband will bring to the average household will be astounding. The holy trinity of communications—voice, video, and data—will all be provided over one connection, from one provider. While these services are being delivered today in areas like Phoenix, Arizona, by cable provider Cox Communications and Qwest Communications, most con-sumers can expect a widespread rollout—and greater speed—within the next five years. . . .

Phone companies, cable operators, and broadband service providers like Santa Clara, California-based Covad Commu-nications are working to speed connectivity. With DSL, for instance, some companies are rolling out delivery of voice, as well as video channels, digital, commercial-free audio sta-tions, and high-speed Internet access—all over one line, with all services operating simultaneously.

As broadband hurtles forward, the networked home of the

future will resemble those that we know from sci-fi movies or cartoons like The Jetsons.

A Wireless World

Wireless devices such as mobile phones and pagers keep us connected with work as well as with family and friends. And a new generation of wireless networks promises to deliver data to handsets at up to 2 million bits per second—more than 100 times what's possible today. At these speeds, service providers like Verizon Wireless, Cingular, AT&T Wireless, and Sprint PCS say that even video will soon be delivered to handsets.

Imagine using a phone not only for getting information from the Internet but also for multimedia games, presentations, and even videoconferencing. The first networks able to offer these services are expected in Europe and Asia by 2002; we can expect deployments by 2003. Why the wait? According to Philip Kendall, mobile communications analyst at Boston-based Strategy Analytics, there are two key reasons. First, the U.S. lags behind most European and Asian countries both in technology and in penetration of the subscriber base. Second, the technology will cost each operator billions of dollars to deploy.

But with rollout expected around 2003, wireless providers will know the exact location of their subscribers. This will allow restaurants, shops, and other retailers to send ads to wireless handsets, enticing users into their stores as they pass. Hungry? A nearby restaurant is offering 10% off dinner via the electronic coupon it just sent to your cell phone.

Mobile handsets will have to evolve even further, of course, combining phone capabilities with elements of personal digital assistants. One example of where the technology is headed is Handspring's Springboard modules for the Visor. The Visor features an expansion slot to add a variety of modules such as a digital camera or the company's VisorPhone, which instantly turns your handheld into a mobile phone.

Handsets like Ericcson's R380 (which comes with a foldout keypad) are already being equipped with larger screens, voice recognition, and greater processing power. And soon handsets will also talk to each other using Bluetooth, a short-range wireless networking technology, says Mark Lowenstein, chief industry strategist at Informico, a wireless Internet infrastructure company based in Lexington, Massachusetts.

Shopping in the Future

In "Store of the Future," Nooshin Ahangar describes plans for making shopping easier and more relaxed. One plan collects merchandise for a customer, and another offers computerized services in a relaxing space with a family room and a kitchen.

In the Buyometrics Store of the Future, Herschman Architects used a computer to recognize shoppers by their faces and to link their identities to information stored in a database. Instead of sifting through merchandise to find the right fit, shoppers can create baskets of merchandise delivered to the fitting rooms. Plasma screens inside the dressing rooms can scan a body into an image that can be e-mailed to friends for feedback before making a purchase. If shoppers like the fit, all they have to do is walk out without having to pass through the register.

Another futuristic concept was introduced by the St. Louis–based telecommunications company Everest. Everest's new retail design looks at interactivity in a relaxed, personal way. The "High Concept" centerpiece unveiled at GlobalShop is not only a model, but a new store is opening in Kansas City, Mo., this summer [2001]. The 2,000-sq. ft. store has a home-like appearance, equipped with telephone services, cable and Internet access. The circular-shaped space was designed with a family room, a playroom, kitchen and home office.

"This type of project has not been done before," says Jerry Birnbach, president of Retail Design and Display of Granite Springs, N.Y., which designed the Everest exhibit. "This company is unique because it offers all three services and when you bundle them all under one bill, you get much more services for less."

Nooshin Ahangar, "Store of the Future," *Display & Design Ideas* 13 (May 2001):62. Copyright © 2001, held by Bill Communications, Inc.

Bluetooth-enabled devices exchange information and synchronize data between handsets and PCs. But with more cars, homes, businesses, and wearable devices—such as Samsung's Watch Style Phone—being outfitted with wireless connections, this technology promises to dramatically change the way we work and communicate. And with dozens of companies involved in the development of this technology (Nokia and Motorola are the two most notable ones), we can expect rollout of Bluetooth-enabled devices by the end of this year [2001].

No More Boxes

These days, shrink-wrapped software packages are passé. If you want software, you get it online. And industry analysts say that five years from now, software will be available only as a download on a rental or subscription basis via application service providers (ASPs). This is already a trend that even Microsoft has acknowledged with its ASP Licensing Program, which permits ASPs to license Microsoft products on a monthly basis.

Corporations and small businesses are clamoring for these services—and, increasingly, so are consumers. ASPs provide applications such as Microsoft Excel, PowerPoint, and Word for a monthly fee; some also offer their own software (like Sun Microsystems' StarOffice 5.2, available as a free download), which is similar to and in most cases compatible with Microsoft applications. ASPs also provide the support services required to deliver and maintain their offerings.

For companies, the lure is the promise of reducing IT costs by 30% to 60%. For consumers, it's a way to try software without being locked into an expensive product as well as costly upgrades; best of all, the software comes with tech support.

Choosing an ASP also saves valuable hardware space, since the applications needed to use an ASP's software are generally a fraction of the size of, say, Microsoft Word or Excel. Additionally, the software is stored on the provider's servers. Because of this, you can access the applications and work remotely, rather than being tied to a desk.

The rental model is attractive, says Chris Whitely, project

manager at Insight Research Corp., a telecom market-research firm in Parsippany, New Jersey. "I think the major pros are that for the software you are less likely to use now, you can use it on a trial or occasional basis."

But, says Whitely, there's a downside. "In effect, customers give up some level of control in exchange for using the applications. It really is a major shift in the way that people are used to getting their software."

Digital Dollars

If you've ever shopped on the Internet—or sold products there—you know that one of the most difficult parts of an online transaction is payment. And while vendors are making it easier to use credit cards online, not everyone is comfortable with the idea. Enter digital cash. Or, rather, reenter digital cash.

Digital cash, an Internet-based payment system, lets users pay individuals and businesses online with real U.S. dollars (not gift certificates or reward points), and send money electronically to actual bank accounts.

If the term sounds familiar, it should. This is actually the second iteration of an Internet digital payment system. The difference between this version and DigiCash, however, is that the original was not actual U.S. currency. DigiCash was like buying a gift certificate and using it at online merchants, similar to, say, Flooz.com.

Although still in its infancy, the current iteration of digital cash is blazing its own trails. Currently, you can send cash via e-mail once you open an account with a provider, enabling you to pay at an online merchant or auction sites. For consumers, there's no fee; merchants typically pay 1% to 2% on each transaction to companies such as PayPal and Check-Free, a bill-payment firm that will roll out its own digital cash service later this year.

PayPal's 4.5 million users send about $7 million daily. Users simply open an account with the company with either a credit card or bank account information. The company also pays 5.2% annual interest on balances. These accounts are not FDIC insured, however.

Home Technology Simplified

With terms like "convergence," "broadband," and "networked home" now commonplace, vendors are seeking to lighten the load on the home front. Does anyone remember WebTV? The newest generation of Web home devices is the best evidence that Internet appliances are here to stay—in some form or another.

Netpliance led the way in 1999 with the iOpener. Currently 3Com is touting Audrey (a digital home assistant), which features a wireless keyboard and a stylus. Compaq is also in the picture, offering the iPAQ Home Internet Appliance.

While these units don't have the processing power and speed of a typical late-model PC, they are widely being accepted for what they can do, and are finding a welcoming audience among those who want the basics—e-mail, Internet access, and home-management tools such as scheduling, address book, and recipe storage. All feature one-touch access to e-mail and the Internet, and are a fraction of the cost of a PC (from $199 to $549, plus Web access).

So what's next for Internet appliances? "Wireless," says Jon Conmy, 3Com's manager of developing applications. "In a home setting, wireless technologies will allow us to more elegantly insert new products easily and more intelligently."

Because consumers will use these appliances for Internet content rather than, say, creating spreadsheets and Word documents, these units going forward will also focus on lifestyle and entertainment features, says Conmy. In fact, 3Com began shipping Kerbango, an Internet radio that can fetch thousands of stations around the globe, in January [2001].

Discussion Questions

Chapter 1: The History and Identification of Computer Technology

1. Gene I. Rochlin states that a number of factors, neither the computer hardware nor the software alone, caused the computer revolution. What factors blended together to cause the rapid growth of computer use?

2. M. David Ermann, Mary B. Williams, and Claudio Gutierrez maintain that the many uses of the computer in business have potential risks and benefits. What risks and benefits do the authors identify? According to the authors, how do the risks balance with the benefits?

3. John G. Nellist and Elliott M. Gilbert point out that many people think the Internet *is* the information superhighway, but the authors say it is only part of the superhighway. What other elements do the authors include? What are the latest developments and the proposed developments in information and communications technology?

4. According to Fred Williams, how does artificial intelligence differ from traditional computer programming? What features of artificial intelligence make it likely to become more widely used in the future of the investment business?

5. According to Carl Zimmer why is Digitalia needed for the study of evolution? What two successful experiments have been conducted so far? What are the limitations of using Digitalia for the study of evolution?

Chapter 2: Technology's Effects on Business and Industry

1. According to Gerard H. Michaud and Richard Burda, why is automating the handling of data a better way to automate a factory than automating equipment? What specific information is collected about the equipment, the process, and the materials?

2. Gregory J.E. Rawlins describes present and future warfare in terms of escalation—in speed, cost, and computer competence. How will each of these factors affect military power?

3. What two roles does Gregory J.E. Rawlins identify for humans

in future wars? Do you think politicians will view future wars as worth fighting?

Chapter 3: Society in the Computer Age

1. What does Michael B. Eisenberg mean when he says that students need "to use technology flexibly and creatively"? What are the major components of the Big6 process, and how are they useful to students and adults?

2. Do you agree with Claudia Orr, David Allen, and Sandra Poindexter that negative attitudes toward using computers are widespread? What solution have the authors found to overcome negative attitudes when they exist?

3. According to Russ B. Altman, what three stages of medicine have benefited from the contributions of artificial intelligence? What does the mapping of the genome have to do with the third stage?

4. Does Andrew L. Shapiro take a positive, negative, or neutral stand regarding virtual communities? Cite evidence from his article to support your conclusion. What does Shapiro recommend to ensure the viability of local communities *and* the attraction of virtual communities?

5. Douglas S. Robertson describes the changes brought by new computer technology as both "nearly invisible" and "a tidal wave." How can the changes be both of these things? How do you think that these changes will affect people of different ages, of different income levels, of different countries?

6. What kinds of crimes against children are made easier with the Internet? What kinds of laws should govern pornography on the Internet? Should virtual child pornography be a crime? Why, or why not? What view does Paul J. Becker take regarding pornography laws?

Chapter 4: The Technology of the Future

1. According to David Siegel, what impact will technology have on the job search in the future? What is a Universal Résumé and how will it benefit both job candidates and managers?

2. David Siegel says that videos are "a win for everyone"—job candidates and employers alike. Do you agree or can you foresee a greater advantage for one or the other?

3. Of the five technologies that Jason P. McKay discusses, which will benefit you the most? McKay mentions no disadvantages or risks with any of the five; do you see any?

4. Jason P. McKay quotes Jon Conmy, predicting that technology will focus on "lifestyle and entertainment features." What specific features do "lifetime" and "entertainment" entail? Do they appeal to you?

Appendix of Documents

Document 1: Critical Issues in the Information Age

In The Road Ahead, *Microsoft founder Bill Gates (with Nathan Myhrvold and Pete Rinearson) expresses optimism about the abundant opportunities created by new computer technology. However, he also identifies concerns: workers' jobs displaced by computers and workers' anxieties about being left behind. These concerns, he believes, will not bother the next generation, who will have grown up with computers.*

This is an exciting time in the Information Age. It is the very beginning. Almost everywhere I go, whether to speak to a group or to have dinner with friends, questions come up about how information technology will change our lives. People want to understand how it will make the future different. Will it make our lives better or worse?

I've already said I'm an optimist, and I'm optimistic about the impact of the new technology. It will enhance leisure time and enrich culture by expanding the distribution of information. It will help relieve pressures on urban areas by enabling individuals to work from home or remote-site offices. It will relieve pressure on natural resources because increasing numbers of products will be able to take the form of bits rather than of manufactured goods. It will give us more control over our lives and allow experiences and products to be custom tailored to our interests. Citizens of the information society will enjoy new opportunities for productivity, learning, and entertainment. Countries that move boldly and in concert with each other will enjoy economic rewards. Whole new markets will emerge, and a myriad of new opportunities for employment will be created. . . .

Just because I'm optimistic doesn't mean I don't have concerns about what is going to happen to all of us. As with all major changes, the benefits of the information society will carry costs. There will be dislocations in some business sectors that will create a need for worker retraining. The availability of virtually free communications and computing will alter the relationships of nations, and of socioeconomic groups within nations. The power and versatility of digital technology will raise new concerns about individual privacy, commercial confidentiality, and national security. There are, moreover, equity issues that will have to be addressed. The information society should serve all of its citizens, not only the technically sophisticated and economically privileged. In short, a range of important issues confronts us. . . .

Perhaps the most widespread and personal anxiety is, "How will I fit into the evolving economy?" Men and women are worried that their own jobs will become obsolete, that they won't be able to adapt to new ways of working, that their children will get into industries that will cease to exist, or that economic upheaval will create wholesale unemployment, especially among older workers. These are legitimate concerns. Entire professions and industries will fade. But new ones will flourish. This will be happening over the next two or three decades, which is fast by historical standards, but may turn out to be no more disruptive than the pace at which the microprocessor revolution brought about its changes in the workplace, or the upheavals in the airline, trucking, and banking industries over the last decade.

Although the microprocessor and the personal computer that it enabled have altered and even eliminated some jobs and companies, it is hard to find any large sector of the economy that has been negatively affected. Mainframe, minicomputer, and typewriter companies have downsized, but the computer industry as a whole has grown, with a substantial net increase in employment. As big computer companies such as IBM or DEC have laid people off, many of those workers have found employment within the industry—usually at companies doing something related to PCs. . . .

More than ever, an education that emphasizes general problem-solving skills will be important. In a changing world, education is the best preparation for being able to adapt. As the economy shifts, people and societies who are appropriately educated will tend to do best. The premium that society pays for skills is going to climb, so my advice is to get a good formal education and then keep on learning. Acquire new interests and skills throughout your life.

A lot of people will be pushed out of their comfort zones, but that doesn't mean that what they already know won't still be valuable. It does mean that people and companies will have to be open to reinventing themselves—possibly more than once. Companies and governments can help train and retrain workers, but the individual must ultimately bear principal responsibility for his education.

A first step will be to come to terms with computers. Computers make almost everyone nervous before they understand them. Children are the primary exception. First-time users worry that a single misstep will cause them to ruin the computer or lose everything stored in it. People do lose data, of course, but very rarely is the damage irreversible. We have worked to make it harder to lose data and easier to recover from mistakes. Most programs have "Undo" commands that make it simple to try something, then quickly reverse it. Users become more confident as they see that making mistakes won't be catastrophic. . . .

Ultimately, the information highway is not for my generation or those before me. It is for future generations. The kids who have grown up with PCs in the last decade, and those who will grow up with the highway in the next, will push the technology to its limits.

We have to pay particular attention to correcting the gender imbalance. When I was young, it seemed that only boys were encouraged to mess around with computers. Girls are far more active with computers today than twenty years ago, but there are still many fewer women in technical careers. By making sure that girls as well as boys become comfortable with computers at an early age we can ensure that they play their rightful role in all the work that benefits from computer expertise.

My own experience as a child, and that of my friends raising children today, is that once a kid is exposed to computing, he or she is hooked. But we have to create the opportunity for that exposure. Schools should have low-cost access to computers connected to the information highway, and teachers need to become comfortable with the new tools.

Bill Gates, with Nathan Myhrvold and Pete Rinearson, *The Road Ahead*. New York: Viking, 1995, pp. 250–58.

Document 2: "A Digital Nervous System"

In Business @ the Speed of Thought, *Microsoft founder Bill Gates (with Collins Hemingway) coins the phrase "a digital nervous system" as a metaphor to describe the way emerging hardware, software, and communication systems will reshape business. Just as the biological nervous system triggers responses, the digital infrastructure will activate information, allow companies to react to the environment, sense needs, and organize responses.*

The job that most companies are doing with information today would have been fine several years ago. Getting rich information was prohibitively expensive, and the tools for analyzing and disseminating it weren't available in the 1980s and even the early 1990s. But here on the edge of the twenty-first century, the tools and connectivity of the digital age now give us a way to easily obtain, share, and act on information in new and remarkable ways.

For the first time, all kinds of information—numbers, text, sound, video—can be put into a digital form that any computer can store, process, and forward. For the first time, standard hardware combined with a standard software platform has created economies of scale that make powerful computing solutions available inexpensively to companies of all sizes. And the "personal" in personal computer means that individual knowledge workers have a powerful tool for analyzing and using the information delivered by these solutions. The microprocessor revolution not only is giving PCs an exponential rise in power, but is on the verge of creating a whole new generation of personal digital companions—handhelds, Auto PCs, smart cards, and others on the way—that will make the use of digital information pervasive. A key to this pervasiveness is the improvement in Internet technologies that are giving us worldwide connectivity.

In the digital age, "connectivity" takes on a broader meaning than simply putting two or more people in touch. The Internet creates a new universal space for information sharing, collaboration, and commerce. It provides a new medium that takes the immediacy and spontaneity of technologies such as the TV and the phone and combines them with the depth and breadth inherent in paper communications. In addition, the ability to find information and match people with common interests is completely new.

These emerging hardware, software, and communications standards will reshape business and consumer behavior. Within a decade most people will regularly use PCs at work and at home, they'll use e-mail routinely, they'll be connected to the Internet, they'll carry digital devices containing their personal and business information. New consumer devices will emerge that handle almost every kind of data—text, numbers, voice, photos, videos—in digital form. I use the phrases "Web workstyle" and "Web lifestyle" to emphasize the impact of employees and consumers taking advantage of these digital connections. Today, we're usually linked to information only when we are at our desks, connected to the Internet by a physical wire. In the future, portable digital devices will keep us constantly in touch with other systems and other people. And everyday devices such as water and electrical meters, security systems, and automobiles will be connected as well, reporting on their usage and status. Each of these applications of digital information is approaching an inflection point—the moment at which change in consumer use becomes sudden and massive. Together they will radically transform our lifestyles and the world of business.

Already, the Web workstyle is changing business processes at Microsoft and other companies. Replacing paper processes with collaborative digital processes has cut weeks out of our budgeting and other operational processes. Groups of people are using electronic tools to act together almost as fast as a single person could act, but with the insights of the entire team. Highly motivated teams are getting the benefit of everyone's thinking. With faster access to information about our sales, our partner activities, and, most important, our customers, we are able to react faster to problems and opportunities. Other pioneering companies going digital are achieving similar breakthroughs.

We have infused our organization with a new level of electronic-based intelligence. I'm not talking about anything metaphysical or about some weird cyborg episode out of *Star Trek*. But it is something new and important. To function in the digital age, we have developed a new digital infrastructure. It's like the human nervous system. The biological nervous system triggers your reflexes so that you can react quickly to danger or need. It gives you the information you need as you ponder issues and make choices. You're alert to the most important things, and your nervous system blocks out the information that isn't important to you. Companies need to have that same kind of nervous system—the ability to run smoothly and efficiently, to respond quickly to emergencies and opportunities, to quickly get valuable information to the people in the company who need it, the ability to quickly make decisions and interact with customers.

As I was considering these issues and putting the final touches on my speech for the CEO summit, a new concept popped into my head: "the digital nervous system." A digital nervous system is the corporate, digital equivalent of the human nervous system, providing a well-integrated flow of information to the right part of the organization at the right time. A digital nervous system consists of the digital processes that enable a company to perceive and react to its environment, to sense competitor challenges and customer needs, and to organize timely responses. A digital nervous system requires a combination of hardware and software; it's distinguished from a mere network of computers by the accuracy, immediacy, and richness of the information it brings to knowledge workers and the *insight* and *collaboration* made possible by the information.

I made the digital nervous system the theme of my talk. My goal was to excite the CEOs about the potential of technology to drive the flow of information and help them run their businesses better. To let them see that if they did a good job on information flow, individual business solutions would come more easily. And because a digital nervous system benefits every department and individual in the company, I wanted to make them see that only they, the CEOs, could step up to the change in mind-set and culture necessary to reorient a company's behavior around digital information flow and the Web workstyle. Stepping up to such a decision meant that they had to become comfortable enough with digital technology to understand how it could fundamentally change their business processes.

Bill Gates, with Collins Hemingway, *Business @ the Speed of Thought: Using a Digital Nervous System*. New York: Warner Books, 1999, pp. xv–xviii.

Document 3: Comparison of the Industrial and Information Societies

Japanese writer Yoneji Masuda argues that the information society will be very different from, though not necessarily better or worse than, the industrial society. In his book, The Information Society as Post-Industrial Society, *he includes this chart to highlight the differences.*

Pattern comparison of industrial society and the information society

	Industrial society	Information society
Innovational technology		
Core	Steam engine (power)	Computer (memory, computation, control)
Basic function	Replacement, amplification of physical labor	Replacement, amplification of mental labor
Productive power	Material productive power (increase in per capita production)	Information productive power (increase in optimal action–selection capabilities)
Socio-economic structure		
Products	Useful goods and services	Information, technology, knowledge
Production center	Modern factory (machinery, equipment)	Information utility (information networks, data banks)
Market	New world, colonies, consumer purchasing power	Increase in knowledge frontiers, information space
Leading industries	Manufacturing industries (machinery industry, chemical industry)	Intellectual industries, (information industry, knowledge industry)
Industrial structure	Primary, secondary, tertiary industries	Matrix industrial structure (primary, secondary, tertiary, quaternary/systems industries)
Economic structure	Commodity economy (division of labor, separation of production and consumption)	Synergetic economy (joint production and shared utilization)
Socio-economic principle	Law of price (equilibrium of supply and demand)	Law of goals (principle of synergetic feedforward)
Socio-economic	Enterprise (private enterprise,	Voluntary communities (local and

subject	public enterprise, third sector)	informational communities)
Socio-economic system	Private ownership of capital, free competition, profit maximization	Infrastructure, principle of synergy, precedence of social benefit
Form of society	Class society (centralized power, classes, control)	Functional society (multicenter, function, autonomy)
National goal	GNW (gross national welfare)	GNS (gross national satisfaction)
Form of government	Parliamentary democracy	Participatory democracy
Force of social change	Labor movements, strikes	Citizens' movements, litigation
Social problems	Unemployment, war, fascism	Future shock, terror, invasion of privacy
Most advanced stage	High mass consumption	High mass knowledge creation

Values

Value standards	Material values (satisfaction of physiological needs)	Time-value (satisfaction of goal achievement needs)
Ethical standards	Fundamental human rights, humanity	Self-discipline, social contribution
Spirit of the times	Renaissance (human liberation)	Globalism (symbiosis of man and nature)

Yoneji Masuda, *The Information Society as Post-Industrial Society*. Bethesda, MD: World Future Society, 1981 and 1983, in Tom Forester, ed., *The Information Technology Revolution*. Cambridge, MA: MIT Press, 1985, p. 622.

Document 4: An Ethical Code for Computer Professionals

Members of the Association for Computing Machinery have developed a code of ethics and set guidelines for professional conduct. Published in Communications of the ACM, *the code and guidelines serve as a basis for decision making and for judging complaints when standards have been violated.*

Preamble. Commitment to ethical professional conduct is expected of every member (voting members, associate members, and student members) of the Association for Computing Machinery (ACM).

This Code, consisting of 24 imperatives formulated as statements of personal responsibility, identifies the elements of such a commitment. It contains many, but not all, issues professionals are likely to face. Section 1 outlines fundamental ethical considerations, while Section 2 addresses additional, more specific considerations of professional conduct. Statements in Section 3 pertain more specifically to individuals who have a leadership role, whether in the workplace or in a volunteer capacity such as with organizations like ACM. Principles involving compliance with this Code are given in Section 4.

The Code shall be supplemented by a set of Guidelines, which provide explanation to assist members in dealing with the various issues contained in the Code. It is expected that the Guidelines will be changed more frequently than the Code.

The Code and its supplemented Guidelines are intended to serve as a basis for ethical decision making in the conduct of professional work. Secondarily, they may serve as a basis for judging the merit of a formal complaint pertaining to violation of professional ethical standards. It should be noted that although computing is not mentioned in the imperatives of Section 1, the Code is concerned with how these fundamental imperatives apply to one's conduct as a computing professional. These imperatives are expressed in a general form to emphasize that ethical principles that apply to computer ethics are derived from more general ethical principles.

It is understood that some words and phrases in a code of ethics are subject to varying interpretations, and that any ethical principle may conflict with other ethical principles in specific situations. Questions related to ethical conflicts can best be answered by thoughtful consideration of fundamental principles, rather than reliance on detailed regulations.

1. GENERAL MORAL IMPERATIVES

As an ACM member I will . . .

1.1 Contribute to society and human well-being.

1.2 Avoid harm to others.

1.3 Be honest and trustworthy.

1.4 Be fair and take action not to discriminate.

1.5 Honor property rights including copyrights and patents.

1.6 Give proper credit for intellectual property.

1.7 Respect the privacy of others.

1.8 Honor confidentiality.

2. MORE SPECIFIC PROFESSIONAL RESPONSIBILITIES

As an ACM computing professional I will . . .

2.1 Strive to achieve the highest quality, effectiveness, and dignity in both the process and products of professional work.

2.2 Acquire and maintain professional competence.

2.3 Know and respect existing laws pertaining to professional work.

2.4 Accept and provide appropriate professional review.

2.5 Give comprehensive and thorough evaluations of computer systems and their impacts, including analysis of possible risks.

2.6 Honor contracts, agreements, and assigned responsibilities.

2.7 Improve public understanding of computing and its consequences.

2.8 Access computing and communication resources only when authorized to do so.

3. ORGANIZATIONAL LEADERSHIP IMPERATIVES

As an ACM member and an organizational leader, I will . . .

3.1 Articulate social responsibilities of members of an organizational unit and encourage full acceptance of those responsibilities.

3.2 Manage personnel and resources to design and build information systems that enhance the quality of working life.

3.3 Acknowledge and support proper and authorized uses of an organization's computing and communication resources.

3.4 Ensure that users and those who will be affected by a system have their needs clearly articulated during the assessment and design of requirements; later the system must be validated to meet requirements.

3.5 Articulate and support policies that protect the dignity of users and others affected by a computing system.

3.6 Create opportunities for members of the organization to learn the principles and limitations of computer systems.

4. COMPLIANCE WITH THE CODE

As an ACM member, I will . . .

4.1 Uphold and promote the principles of this Code.

4.2 Treat violations of this code as inconsistent with membership in the ACM.

"Code of Ethics and Professional Conduct (1992)," in Rob Kling, ed., *Computerization and Controversy: Value Conflicts and Social Choices.* 2nd ed. San Diego: Academic Press, 1996, pp. 878–80.

Document 5: Privacy Bills Proposed by Congress

The following table presents the legislation relating to computer privacy introduced in the 106th Congress, compiled in Data Privacy in the Information Age, *by Jacqueline Klosek. Two sources prompted congressional action: News stories reporting privacy problems and pressure from the European community for the United States to pass stronger privacy laws. As a result of the proposed bills, private industry has explored self-regulatory measures.*

Table of Privacy-Related Bills Proposed in the 106th Congress
House of Representatives Bills

Bill Number and Title	Brief Description
H.R. 10 Financial Services Act of 1999	Requires FTC to issue interim reports on consumer privacy.
H.R. 30 Financial Information Privacy Act of 1999	To protect consumers and financial institutions by preventing personal financial information from being obtained from financial institutions under false pretenses.
H.R. 97 Personal Privacy Protection Act	Prohibits physical intrusion into privacy for commercial purposes.
H.R. 220 Freedom and Privacy Restoration Act of 1999	Limits the use of social security numbers and prohibits the creation of governmental identification cards.
H.R. 313 Consumer Internet Privacy Protection Act of 1999	Regulates the use of interactive computer services of personally identifiable information provided by subscribers to such services.
H.R. 385 Patients' Bill of Rights of 1999	Requires health plans and insurers to protection confidentiality of medical records and allows patient access.
H.R. 367 Social Security Online Privacy Protection Act of 1999	Limits disclosure of social security numbers by interactive computer services.
H.R. 369 Children's Privacy Protection and Parental Empowerment Act of 1999	Prohibits the sale of personal information about children without their parents' consent.
H.R. 448 Patient Protection Act of 1999	Sets rules on confidentiality of health care information.
H.R. 514 Wireless Privacy Enhancement Act of 1999	Prohibits interception of wireless communications.
H.R. 516 "Know Your Customer" Sunset Act	Prohibits government from implementing the "Know Your Customer" rules.
H.R. 517 FinCen Public Accountability Act	Requires FinCen to be subject to the Privacy Act.
H.R. 518 Bank Secrecy Sunset Act	Prohibits government from implementing "Know Your Customer" rules and ends provisions of the Bank Secrecy act that requires disclosure of information to government.
H.R. 530 American Financial Institutions' Privacy Act	Prohibits "Know Your Customer" regulations from going into effect without Act of Congress.
H.R. 575 Know Your Customers Regulation Termination Act	Prohibits "Know Your Customer" regulations from going into effect.
H.R. 575 Know Your Customers Regulation Abolishment Act	Prohibits "Know Your Customer" regulations from going into effect.
H.R. 850 Security and Freedom Through Encryption (SAFE) Act	Relaxes export controls on encryption, prohibits mandatory key escrow and creates criminal penalties for using cryptography in a crime.

H.R. 1057 Medical Information Privacy and Security Act	Sets general rules on use and disclosure of medical records.

Senate Bills

S. 6 Patient's Bill of Rights Act of 1999	Requires health plans and insurers to protect the confidentiality of medical records and to allow patient access.
S. 187 Financial Information Privacy Act of 1999	Requires the FDIC to set privacy rules.
S. 240 Patient's Bill of Rights Act of 1999	Requires health plans and insurers to protect the confidentiality of medical records and allow patient access.
S. 300 Patient's Bill of Rights Plus Act	Sets privacy protections and prohibits genetic discrimination.
S. 326 Patient's Bill of Rights Act	Sets privacy protections and prohibits genetic discrimination.
S. 466 American Financial Institutions Privacy Act of 1999	Prohibits "know your customer" rules unless approved by act of Congress.
S. 573 Medical Information Privacy and Security Act	Provides comprehensive medical privacy protections.
S. 578 Health Care PIN Act	Provides for limited protections on medical records, easy access to records by industry.

Jacqueline Klosek, *Data Privacy in the Information Age*. Westport, CT: Quorum Books, 2000, pp. 144–45.

Document 6: Questioning the Vast Computer Networks

In Silicon Snake Oil: Second Thoughts on the Information Highway, *Clifford Stoll wonders if computer networks are really best seen as "freedom to," or if a real life requires "freedom from" computers.*

The popular mythos tells us that networks are powerful, global, fast, and inexpensive. It's the place to meet friends and carry on business. There, you'll find entertainment, expertise, and education. In short, it's important to be online.

It ain't necessarily so.

Our networks can be frustrating, expensive, unreliable connections that get in the way of useful work. It is an overpromoted, hollow world, devoid of warmth and human kindness.

The heavily promoted information infrastructure addresses few social needs or business concerns. At the same time, it directly threatens precious parts of our society, including schools, libraries, and social institutions.

No birds sing.

For all the promises of virtual communities, it's more important to live a real life in a real neighborhood.

I began this meditation with a perplexed ambivalence toward computers, networks, and the culture that enshrines them.

At first, I wanted to think about technical issues. But I found myself returning to the same themes: real life and authentic experience mean much more than anything the modem can deliver. The culture of information isn't knowledge. Electronic networks erode important parts of our community.

Computer networks, like cars and televisions, confer a most seductive freedom, the "freedom to." As I step back from the insistent messages beckoning from across my computer, I'm beginning to wonder about a different kind of freedom—call it a "freedom from."

Certainly, few will toss out their computers or back away from their keyboards. Our networks are far too useful, and there's so much available over the modem.

Oh?

It's late on an October evening in Oakland; I smell popcorn in the kitchen.

I'm done meditating.

Clifford Stoll, *Silicon Snake Oil: Second Thoughts on the Information Highway*. New York: Doubleday, 1995, pp. 233–34.

Document 7: Frustrations with Automated Calling Systems

In RISKS-FORUM Digest, *R. Aminzade reports a frustrating experience trying to contact AAA road service, and Michael Slavitch reports similar frustration with a library reserve system. Both men had dealt with computerized calling systems that failed.*

Date: Thu, 18 Jan 90 08:24:18 EST
From: R. Aminzade
Subject: Risks of Voice Mail Systems That Expect a Human at the Other End

Last night my car had a dead battery (I left the lights on—something that a very simple piece of digital circuitry could have prevented, but I digress), so I called AAA road service. I noted that they had installed a new digital routing system for phone calls. "If you are cancelling a service call Press 1, if this is an inquiry about an existing service call, Press 2, if this is a new service call, Press 3." All well and good, except that when I finally reached a real operator, she informed me that the towtruck would arrive "within 90 minutes." In less than the proposed hour and a half I managed to beg jumper cables off of an innocent passerby and get the car started, so I decided to call AAA and cancel the service call. I dialed, pressed 1 as instructed, and waited. The reader should realize that my car was illegally parked (this is Boston), running (I wasn't going to get stuck with a dead battery again!), and had the keys in the ignition. I was not patient. I waited about four minutes, then tried again. Same result. I was now out of dimes, but I noticed that the AAA machine began its message with "we will accept your collect call . . ." so I decided to call collect. Surprise! I discovered that New England Telephone had just installed its digital system for collect calls. It is quite sophisticated, using some kind of voice recognition circuit. The caller dials the usual 0-(phone number), and then is asked "If you wish to make a collect call, press 1 . . . If you wish to . . ." Then the recording asks "please say your name." The intended recipient of the collect call then gets a call that begins "Will you accept a collect call from [recording of caller stating his name]." I knew what was coming, but I didn't want to miss this experience. I gave my name as something like "Russell, Goddammit!," and NET's machine began asking AAA's machine if it would accept a collect call (which it had already, plain to the human ear, said it would accept) from "Russell Goddammit!" Ms. NET (why are these always female voices?) kept telling Ms. AAA "I'm sorry, I don't understand you, please answer yes or no," but Ms. AAA went blithely on with her shpiel, instructing Ms. NET which buttons to push. I stood at the phone (car still running . . . machines nattering away at each other) wondering who could do this episode justice. Kafka? Orwell? Groucho? I was sure that one machine or the other would eventually give up and turn things over to a human being, but, I finally decided to dial a human operator, and subject the poor woman to a stream of abuse. She connected me to AAA, where I punched 3 (rather than the appropriate but obviously malfunctioning 1), and subjected yet another unpaid clerk to my wrath.

Date: Mon, 7 Nov 94 15:45:50 -0500
From: Michael Slavitch, Consultant, (613) 781-9824
<slavitche@on.bell.ca>
Subject: Ottawa Library Fines People Using Unreliable Automatic Calling System

About two months ago I reserved a book at my local library. The library has gone electronic in its reservation system. You reserve a book, and when your turn to receive it comes due a computer dials your home phone number. If an answer occurs, it assumes you heard the message; if you do not pick up the book in three days, you are fined $2.00.

Basically, this is what happened to me. Their computer called my number and the phone went off hook, starting the meter running. For some reason my answering machine did not pick up the message (I have an answering machine and a fax modem hanging off the same line, but the fax modem is outgoing only).

The RISK here is obvious, and I consider it nontrivial. The librarian insisted that the "system" is "reliable" and "almost always" works. Well, my knowledge of datacomm says that if it does not always work it is not reliable, and that they are fining people based on an assumption that the message was received.

What's scary was the attitude of the librarian. Because she was told by someone that the system works, she insisted that I had received the call. I asked her for proof of that and she said that "the system said you got the call, it must be true." My attempt to describe the essence of data communications and reliable communication fell on deaf ears, and she refused to give me the name of her superior because "the system works and nobody should complain about it."

Well, I am. I know that it is only two bucks, but the implications that arise from misuse or overly trusting such a system are worrisome. What if the government started issuing parking tickets or summonses in this manner, or banks warned you of surcharges on financial transactions? What if my wife answered the phone and the book was "How to Handle Infidelity in Your Marriage" :) (it wasn't)?

So how do you handle two things?:

[One] An unreliable delivery system being assumed to be reliable.

[Two] People placing trust in such a system.

R. Aminzade and Michael Slavitch, "*RISKS-FORUM* Digest Contributions." In Rob Kling, ed., *Computerization and Controversy: Value Conflicts and Social Choices.* 2nd ed. San Diego, Academic Press, 1996, pp. 764–66.

Document 8: A Computer Utopia

The first computer developers in California envisioned a world in which advanced high technology merged with a simple bucolic life. In The Cult of Information, *Theodore Roszak describes this ideal.*

Utopian visions of the future have generally been divided between two philosophical camps. The first—it might be called the *reversionary* scenario—has begun by wishing the industrial world away. The nineteenth century socialist leader and artist William Morris typifies this viewpoint. Anguished by the moral horrors of Victorian factory life and the aesthetic horrors of mass production,

Morris (in his *News from Nowhere*) envisaged a postindustrial future that recreated the preindustrial past, a society of villages, family farms, and tribal settlements. His ideal economy was based on the handicrafts; government was an informal communal arrangement among virtuous bucolics.

In contrast, other utopians—the *technophiles*—have enthusiastically embraced the urban-industrial system, hoping to see it mature into a wholly new order of life in which science and technology have permanently mastered the forces of nature and have undertaken to redesign the planet. This is the future predicted by Francis Bacon in his *New Atlantis* and by H.G. Wells in his *Shape of Things To Come*.

The future which the guerrilla hackers envisioned is unique in its determination to synthesize these two seemingly contradictory images. They wanted to have it both ways. Committed by their tastes and talents to the expansion of high tech, they had no hesitation in seeking to play through the full repertory of computer electronics and global telecommunications. But the new technology would be contained within an organic and communitarian political context. Somehow the folksy, funky ways of the Homebrew Computer Club and Community Memory would be preserved. Things would be kept decentralized and humanly scaled; indeed, the computer would make that very result possible. It would undergird a new Jeffersonian democracy based, not upon the equal distribution of land, but upon equal access to information. The destiny of the microcomputer was to create a global culture of electronic villages cradled in a healthy natural environment—the sort of world one found scattered through the pages of the *Whole Earth Catalog*. In this charming and idealistic scenario, one pictures the computer terminal as a sort of hearth or campfire around which, by way of their modems and satellite transmitters, the clans gather to exchange gossip and graffiti with their counterparts half a world away. So rustic was some of the imagery of this worldview that one might almost believe the computer was a new kind of plow.

Theodore Roszak, *The Cult of Information: The Folklore of Computers and the True Art of Thinking*. New York: Pantheon, 1986, pp. 146–48.

Document 9: Steve Wozniak and Steven Jobs, Cofounders of Apple Computer

In Steve Wozniak: Inventor of the Apple Computer, *Martha E. Kendall explains how the personal computer got its start. Steve Wozniak was a member of the Homebrew Computer Club, a now-famous frater-*

nity of computer enthusiasts who met to exchange ideas. Wozniak had designed and built an easy-to-use circuit board, which he called a computer, and displayed it at a Homebrew meeting. Steven Jobs saw it there; certain that others would want one, he took orders for one hundred computers, which the two engineers made in the garage of Jobs's home, the seed of Apple Computer, Inc.

Steve Wozniak and Steve Jobs were just two examples of the many talented engineers who virtually lived and breathed the new technology. Although they worked at various locations throughout Silicon Valley, these engineers craved an opportunity to meet and swap ideas, to pool their knowledge, and to discuss their discoveries and projects. In 1975, Gordon French, a well-respected and successful computer systems designer, finally got this group together. He organized the Homebrew Computer Club, which met in his garage.

Homebrewers ranged from conservatively dressed gray-haired engineers to bearded young men wearing jeans and work shirts. Both professionals and hobbyists who were plugged into the electronic grapevine came to see what was going on. The club grew so popular that after a few meetings it became obvious that the members needed a place larger than French's garage. The auditorium at Stanford's Linear Accelerator Center was available for big groups, so they started meeting there on the second Wednesday of every month. . . .

At Homebrew meetings, Steve [Wozniak] heard about the first personal computers being offered as mail-order kits. These were intended for serious hobbyists and experts like Steve who loved electronics and knew how to assemble sophisticated components. But Steve wanted to design his own.

Daydreaming, he considered the features he wanted his computer to have. It should be easy to program and include what he called "the fun things"—like games. Also, Steve wanted to use his computer to test logic ideas for H-P [Hewlitt-Packard] calculators he was helping to develop. Finally, it had to be a computer he could afford to build. Fortunately, the price of *microprocessors*, which he would need to use in the construction, was coming down, so his dream computer wasn't that far out of his reach. Before long, he would design a computer so easy to use and so affordable that it would eventually find its way into the homes of Americans all across the country—and make him a millionaire in the process. . . .

Steve continued to work at H-P but experienced some disappointment: He was not assigned to work on a programmable computer terminal because he lacked a college degree. After hours, he began building a circuit board for his own ideal computer.

Steve and [high-school classmate] Allen Baum had written a BASIC programming language for a Motorola 68,000 microprocessor, and Steve had designed a circuit board to run it. Now Steve substituted a new microprocessor from MOS Technology, called the 6502, almost exactly the same as the Motorola one but cheaper and easier to find. Proud and excited about creating this improved circuit board, Steve took it to Homebrew meetings. He was happy both to show it off to his friends and to let them use his plans in their own projects.

Steve and his friends called the circuit board itself the "computer." After putting the circuit board together, they would connect it to a TV (which functioned as the computer's monitor), power supply, transformers, and a keyboard so the whole thing could operate, using programs they wrote themselves.

When Steve Jobs saw Steve's computer, he thought that many people would want one just like it. As he had done with the blue boxes (an earlier business venture), Jobs saw a business opportunity and was ready to go for it.

Determined to translate Steve's design into dollars, Steve Jobs urged his friend to start a company with him. But Woz (Steve Wozniak's nickname) had no particular desire to do so; he still liked working at H-P and didn't want to leave. Having designed his computer during his spare time, he figured he could continue working on similar projects as a sideline. Steve Jobs continued to pressure him, however, and Steve eventually agreed to work with Jobs—he had a hard time saying no to anyone. But he would not agree to leave H-P.

In order to start, they had to take care of a few details. First, what would they call the new computer? They wanted a name that reflected its break with tradition. It was not made with big business in mind: it was a labor of love produced by a genius who enjoyed electronics, games, and programming. The name needed to convey their fresh attitude, something new and healthy. A few years earlier, in a search for new ideas and philosophies, Steve Jobs had traveled to India, where he had tried vegetarianism and had worked in an apple orchard. How about "Apple" for the name?

Name a computer after a fruit? Was this another prank? Yes and no. On April Fool's Day, 1976, they officially formed the Apple Computer Company. Steve Wozniak was twenty-six years old; Steve Jobs was twenty-one.

Apple had a name, but it also needed money. They sold Steve Jobs's Volkswagen van and Steve's programmable calculator, raising a total of $1,350. Jobs could ride his bike, and Woz could borrow a calculator when he needed one.

Besides cash, they needed something else: a place to produce the circuit boards. They settled on the garage at Jobs's family home. This location fit within the burgeoning tradition of new companies in Silicon Valley. . . .

Apple Computer Inc. was established in January 1977 by Steve Wozniak, Steve Jobs, and Mike Markkula. The trio lost no time in launching Markkula's ambitious business plan, which called for rapid growth in every area. With Steve's innovative Apple II design, as well as the financing needed for building and promoting the computer, they were fired with optimism about the new corporation. And in less than two years, Apple's performance would exceed even their high expectations.

Martha E. Kendall, *Steve Wozniak: Inventor of the Apple Computer.* New York: Walker, 1994, pp. 27–32.

Document 10: Bill Gates, Founder of Microsoft

Bill Gates learned to program computers as a teenager with the same energy, daring, and brilliance that he exhibited when he built Microsoft into the largest computer company in the world. In excerpts from American Computer Pioneers, *Mary Northrup selects details that convey the personality and business acumen of Bill Gates.*

The news spread quickly among the students at Lakeside. There was a computer in the school! For Bill Gates, an eighth grader in 1968, this was great news. Computers, rare in schools at the time, gave him a new challenge. Learning about programming was fun for Gates. Soon he was spending all of his free time at the computer.

Even as a teenager, Gates knew enough about computers to start a company. By the time he was nineteen he and a partner had formed Microsoft, which would become the biggest software company ever. . . .

Bill, nicknamed "Trey" for "the third" in his name, was a very bright boy. Grade school often bored him. He earned good grades in math and reading, which he liked. Yet in classes in which he was not interested, he made C's and D's. And he was full of energy.

[Bill's parents] William Jr. and Mary searched for activities for their son. He joined Boy Scouts, learned tennis and skiing, had a paper route, and spent active summers with friends. His parents, worried about increasing behavior problems at school, entered him in Lakeside, an all-boys' private school. There, small gawky Bill, "a nerd before the term was invented," as a teacher remembered him, came into his own. The computer helped. . . .

Gates and fellow student Paul Allen soon passed their teachers in computer knowledge. They cut classes to use the machine. They wanted to learn everything they could about it. This was not at all like a modern personal computer (PC). No screen displayed what was typed. Students worked at a keyboard and a teletype printer. Gates remembers: "I wrote my first software program when I was thirteen years old. It was for playing tic-tac-toe. The computer I was using was huge and cumbersome and slow and absolutely compelling." . . .

One day Allen showed Gates an ad for an Intel chip. The boys bought the 8008 chip for $360. Gates had a plan: "We thought we could use the 8008 as the heart of a special computer to do traffic-volume-count analysis. We were going to make the machines and sell them to traffic departments. So we set up our first company, which we called Traf-O-Data."

They did sell some units. Then sales dropped when buyers found out the company was run by teens. But Traf-O-Data taught the partners much about microprocessors and business. . . .

Gates remembers reading about that first personal computer: ". . . Paul and I didn't know exactly how it would be used, but we were sure it would change us and the world of computing. We were right."

They decided to start a software company. They began to write a program for the Altair. Gates went on leave from Harvard. With lots of work and little sleep, they exhausted themselves.

Without even seeing an Altair, the two wrote BASIC (a computer language) for it. They called Ed Roberts, founder of MITS, the company that built the Altair. Gates told him what they had done. Allen took the program to Albuquerque, New Mexico, home of MITS.

Would it work? The program, on punched paper tape, was fed into the computer. As Allen and Roberts watched, the word READY came out of the printing device. Gates's eight thousand lines of code had done it! Roberts, ready to sell BASIC with his machine, hired Allen. Gates also moved to Albuquerque. They worked to improve their product.

Microsoft Corporation was in business. Their contract with MITS let Gates and Allen own their software as it was leased to users. Gates realized that they were at the beginning of a revolution: "By the time we got to Albuquerque to start Microsoft in 1975, the notion was fairly clear to us that computers were going to be a big, big personal tool."

In the early days of the company they wrote software for other computers, too, and sold hardware. The home computer industry grew explosively, and Microsoft with it. In 1979 the company moved to Bellevue, Washington.

A deal with IBM in 1980 made both companies big players in the personal computer market. Microsoft wrote Microsoft® Disk Operating System (MS-DOS) for IBM. Other companies bought licenses for it, benefiting IBM and Microsoft.

Gates was brilliant and ambitious. He also had an instant-recall memory and the ability to understand the law, which helped in business. His programmers worked the way he did: long hours, seven days a week, forgetting to eat, sometimes sleeping on the office floor. They were a close-knit group. . . .

Microsoft grew at an incredible rate. In 1986 it moved to Redmond, Washington, its current location. By the time he was thirty-one, Gates was a billionaire. . . .

Microsoft's mission was "A computer on every desk and in every home." With multimedia CD-ROMs and programs such as Microsoft® Windows, he commanded the leading software company in the world. Gates was achieving his goal.

Mary Northrup, *American Computer Pioneers.* Springfield, NJ: Enslow, 1998, pp. 65–73.

Document 11: Andy Grove, CEO of Intel

In excerpts from Inside Intel, *Tim Jackson shows the dramatic rise of Andy Grove between 1956, when Andy arrived in the United States as a Hungarian refugee, and 1996, when, as CEO of Intel, the world's most powerful chip company, he delivered the keynote address at the computer industry's most important trade show. Despite his success and new style, he retained an element of his former shyness and reserve.*

A Hungarian refugee who anglicized his name after arriving in the United States by boat in 1956, Andy Grove is one of the most extraordinary figures in American business. He is brilliantly intelligent and articulate, driven, obsessive, neat, and disciplined. Intel has been built in his image. The values taught in the company's private "university"—directness in confronting problems and extreme rationality in approaching management questions—are an extension of Grove's own personality.

Andy Grove's slogan—some have called it "Grove's law"—is

"only the paranoid survive." Daily life inside Intel follows this maxim to the full. By comparison with Microsoft, the company is almost obsessively secretive. The house joke is that its photocopiers are fed with paper that is already marked "Intel Confidential" at the top of every page. The company also operates a security department whose job is surveillance not only of competitors or thieves who might harm Intel's interests but also of the company's own employees. This department has several times crossed the boundaries of what is considered proper behavior in U.S. corporate life.

In a recent book, Grove claims to have elevated paranoia to a tool of management. He argues that it helps companies to watch out for dramatic changes in the business environment that faces them. . . .

In November 1996, Andy Grove delivered a keynote speech at Comdex, the computer industry's leading trade show. His speech—more of an all-singing, all-dancing multimedia presentation than a mere speech—combined a celebration of the quarter century that had passed since the launch of Intel's first microprocessor with a set of predictions of where Grove believed computer technology was heading.

With TV-quality video and movie-theater sound, the presentation was a powerful illustration of how far the technology had progressed since the days of the 4004. More interestingly, it illustrated the distance that Grove himself had traveled. Gone were the thick glasses, gold chains, and Art Garfunkel hairstyle of his 1970s persona. In their place was the 1996-vintage Andy Grove: clipped, tanned, mountain-bike-lean, and with an accent that was more a reminder of an exotic past than a barrier to comprehension. Speaking without any sign of an autocue, Grove delivered his pitch with high speed and fluency. The presentation was designed like a segment from a chat show: it included movie clips, a conversation with a "special guest" from Starbucks Coffee Company on a set gussied up to look like the café of the future, and a computer demo with a technology marketing guy from Intel who had a ponytail.

Andy Grove had arrived. No longer was he the earnest, socially inept physicist who knew exactly how to get a semiconductor fab [process] working smoothly but was at a loss when his secretary burst into tears. Now he was a celebrity—celebrated on the covers of business magazines, adored by the Intel shareholders to whom he had delivered 40 percent annual returns over his decade at the company's helm, and rich beyond most people's dreams. It was true that Gordon Moore, with the benefit of a large stake in Intel from the company's inception, was worth twenty times what Andy

Grove was. But his Intel stock options allowed Grove to clear nearly $95 million in 1996 alone. By most people's standards, that was rich. Sweetest of all, Grove was now out of the shadow of Intel's two founders. There had never been rivalry or tension with Gordon Moore. But it was nice, after years of being the back-office guy who did all the unpleasant jobs while Bob Noyce basked in the sun, to be so widely recognized as the principal architect of Intel's glory.

There were drawbacks to being a public figure. When Terry Gross of National Public Radio's Fresh Air invited Grove on to her program to discuss what he'd said about management in his new book *Only the Paranoid Survive*, the Intel CEO found himself being asked about his family background—and hated it.

GROSS: You grew up in World War II, and I'm wondering how your family was affected.

(Pause)

GROSS [again]: Are you Jewish?

GROVE: Unn-hmm. Yes.

GROSS: Did you have to hide during the war?

GROVE: Unn-hmm. Yes.

GROSS: Was your whole family successful in hiding, or did you have family that was unsuccessful?

GROVE: Well, I don't want to get into the details of it. But some of my family survived and others didn't.

GROSS: You were one of the people who—after managing to survive the Nazis, then Stalin invaded Hungary—you were stuck with communism.

(Pause)

GROVE: Unn-hmm. . . .

To be fair, the transformation from statistician and detail merchant to media star and high-tech visionary was incomplete. During his Comdex presentation, the Intel CEO looked uncomfortable amidst the glitz. His delivery was oddly flat—almost as if a slightly cocky lighting engineer had been asked to take over from David Letterman for the evening. But Andy Grove was clearly learning, just as he always had. It wouldn't take him too long to pick up the skills needed for his new role.

At the height of the Pentium incident, it had been hard to imagine Intel without Grove—or Grove without Intel. After the Comdex speech, the world began to look different. Grove, now sixty, succeeded Gordon Moore as Intel's chairman in May 1997, handing over the presidency of the company to Craig Barrett. In the press release announcing the change, Grove was quoted as saying: "Craig is the guy who keeps the Intel machine running. He is the architect of our manufacturing system, and the principal driver behind our management methods and culture." Significantly, however, Grove retained the title of CEO. But the day was clearly drawing closer when he could retire from Intel and devote himself to skiing, teaching his business school students at Stanford, riding his mountain bike, and spending time with his friends and family in carefully programmed one-on-ones.

Inside St. Paul's Cathedral in London lies the tomb of Sir Christopher Wren, the man who built not only the cathedral itself but also much of the rest of the London skyline after the Great Fire of 1666. Instead of trying to compete with the spectacular sculptures on other tombs nearby, those who were responsible for commemorating Wren, the greatest English architect of the seventeenth century, chose a simple tombstone. On the stone is carved the Latin motto *si monumentum requiris, circumspice*—"If you seek a monument, look around you."

Andy Grove is in a similar situation. The legacy that he leaves behind him is visible throughout the world, in hundreds of millions of personal computers powered by Intel processors. Intel may be second to Microsoft in its power in the industry, but it is considerably more profitable and more profitable than all its customers put together. As well as delivering spectacular returns to shareholders, Intel has also done well by its employees. The company does not publish figures of how many millionaires it has created, but the doubling of the Intel stock price that began in mid-1996 has meant that scores of middle managers inside the company, and possibly hundreds, have made more than enough money to retire on. The decision to extend the company's stock option scheme to all its employees in 1997 came after a spectacular year in which Intel paid out profit-sharing and retirement contributions of $820 million to its staff.

Tim Jackson, *Inside Intel: Andy Grove and the Rise of the World's Most Powerful Chip Company.* New York: Dutton, 1997, pp. 10, 375–78.

Document 12: Steve Case, Boss at AOL

In excerpts from aol.com: How Steve Case Beat Bill Gates, Nailed the Netheads, and Made Millions in the War for the Web, *Kara Swisher shows how Steve Case's bland, steady personality mirrors the characteristics of AOL. By making the America Online website middle-of-the-road, with a clean design that is easy to use, Steve Case drew millions of customers and led the company to its position as the number-one website.*

[Steve] Case—a deliberate and quiet person given to saying little and observing a lot—needed a little light-headedness. He had grown tall and solid, had a mop of dark hair, boyish features, and a decidedly preppy demeanor. He looked like a cardboard cutout of a typical eager young executive on the rise. . . .

His resume thus far was typical of many earnest college graduates from suburban families, except perhaps that he had grown up in the more exotic locale of Honolulu, Hawaii. . . .

Life in the Case family was full of white-bread activities such as Cub Scouts, Little League, and stamp collecting. "Steve was always an easy child, very self-sufficient in everything he did," said [his mother] Carol. "He would quietly watch everyone. . . . I guess you could say that still waters run deep.". . .

Case ultimately decided on his father's alma mater, Williams College, tucked in the northwest corner of Massachusetts. . . .

He was a B-minus student, taking mostly political science courses, but also dabbling in others. His least favorite course was computer programming. Case hated the punch cards and the confusing techspeak. Only one feature intrigued him: the ability of the college's computers to talk to others located elsewhere. "The faraway connections seemed magical," Case remembers. "It struck me as the most completely obvious use for them, and the rest was just for computer wonks.". . .

[Years later] even though AOL was now a public company and its executives had gotten rich in the public offering, it was hardly well-known, still very small, and underfunded. And, there was always the question of whether it would survive, given that its competitors included the massive CompuServe and Prodigy. . . .

The office of the man in charge—Steve Case—was located only ten feet from the drab little lobby. Through the glass, you could actually see him tapping away on a computer. "It probably made a favorable impression, because it said he was not egotistical," said [*Wall Street Journal* reporter Walt] Mossberg. "But it also said this was no major corporation that was going to blow anyone away."

Instead, within minutes, the columnist found himself listening to Case—who, in a baggy Hawaiian shirt, looked more like a college student than an executive. Case immediately told the incredulous Mossberg that AOL would soon be the biggest online service in the world and, later, would become a huge multimedia empire.

While AOL was small enough in those days that a visit from a reporter from *The Wall Street Journal* was a pretty big deal, Case kept up his cocky banter with Mossberg, played on a Macintosh on his desk, and detailed his ambitious plans to beat competitors who had millions of users. Unlike the ad-laden and shopping-oriented Prodigy, AOL would focus on chat and community. Unlike the information-rich but staid CompuServe, AOL would be simple and sexy-looking.

"Without blinking, he said he was going to blow away all the other competitors," said Mossberg. "He was almost morally certain."

Mossberg only shook his head and laughed at the audaciousness of Case's plans for AOL. It was an interesting little company, to be sure, with much more of a free-wheeling feel than the government-oriented companies he had encountered in northern Virginia's sprawling suburbs. And it was definitely much more entrepreneurial than CompuServe and Prodigy. AOL was most certainly a scrapper, thought Mossberg, but he wasn't sure that it was equipped to blow away anything more than its funding. . . .

If you look at Steve Case long enough, you realize finally that he looks like a bit of a blank slate. Perhaps it is because his face is such a placid one. It is not often that you will see a strong emotion cross it—not anger, not joy, not sadness.

So what you see there, in the end, is whatever you want.

And if you listen to Steve Case long enough, you realize that what he is saying is always a variation of exactly the same theme. Perhaps it is because his voice remains modulated and calm—almost robotic like an animatronic dummy at Disneyland. His points come out in full paragraphs, often sounding dry or even a bit dull. Over and over, he describes the same vision of a vast online community.

So what you hear, in the end, is whatever you want.

You recall a flip and thoughtless comment by an editor who once told you he did not like AOL because it was so middle-of-the-road, so bland, so vanilla.

And it finally hits you—that is why AOL has managed, over the years, to survive vicious cycles of trouble; to keep standing, where others have fallen; to prosper, when those thought to be knowledgeable about such things had predicted its demise.

Because Steve Case—and, by extension, AOL—is so middle-of-the-road, so bland, so vanilla. AOL's sites might not win design awards, but they are clean and easy to navigate; the conversations in its chat rooms may seem nearly mind-numbing to some digerati, but they are probably a lot closer to the mundane lives of most Americans; its technology might not be the fastest or coolest or hottest, but, for the most part, it is pretty easy to work and eventually catches up (though recent e-mail lapses are becoming almost inexcusable).

As politicians will tell you, being average is not a bad way to be. . . .

As AOL hits its 11-million-member mark early in 1998 (the figure did not include the millions of expected CompuServe additions) and polls were showing that AOL was the number one Web site accessed from home, Steve Case still remained restless. Even the fortune of close to $400 million he had accumulated had not pacified Case. . . .

Case has been amused to hear that the mood of Silicon Valley—which was altogether snide about AOL only six months before—has become admiring. But he continues to show frustration because people want to celebrate now.

Case does not, throwing out a series of clichés to describe where the company is at this point in time. There's still many more innings to play—we're perhaps at the bottom of the second or the third, he said. This is a marathon, not a sprint, he noted. It takes 10 to 20 years to build a mass market, he insisted, it doesn't just happen overnight.

But, he added, his internal anchor is consistent, as it has always been.

"When people ask me why or how I did it, it's like asking a basketball player, 'Why do you play basketball?,'" said Case, who would doubtless prefer to keep such thoughts of personal motivation mostly to himself. "Probably because you want to be the best."

He was simply curious about the online world, he finally volunteered, and wanted to play a defining role in making it become a real mass medium.

Kara Swisher, *aol.com: How Steve Case Beat Bill Gates, Nailed the Netheads, and Made Millions in the War for the Web.* New York: Times Books, 1998, pp. 24–25, 64–65, 308–309, 317–18.

Chronology

1821
Charles Babbage designs the prototype for the "difference engine," his first mechanical computer.

1836
Using punch cards, Babbage begins to design his "analytical engine," a machine that could perform an addition in three seconds and a multiplication or division in two to four minutes.

1937
English mathematician Alan M. Turing publishes a mathematical theory of computation, solving the problem of reasoning in proposing the simplified computer known as a Turing machine.

1943
Howard H. Aiken and his team build the Harvard Mark I, the first program-controlled calculator, a machine 51 feet long, weighing 3 tons, and incorporating 750,000 parts; Thomas Flowers builds Colossus, the earliest programmable electronic computer, at the Post Office Research Laboratories in London; Colossus contained 2,400 vacuum tubes for logic.

1946
John W. Mauchly and J. Presper Eckert develop the ENIAC (Electronic Numerical Integrator and Computer), one of the first electronic, valve-driven, digital computers; ENIAC weighs 30 tons, contains 18,000 electronic valves, performs 100,000 calculations per second, and is used for calculating ballistic trajectories and testing theories involving the hydrogen bomb.

1947
American physicists William B. Shockley, John Bardeen, and Walter H. Brattain invent the transistor at the Bell Telephone Laboratories.

1948
SSEM (Small Scale Experimental Machine), the first computer to store both the program and data in RAM, is built at Manchester University in England.

1949

First computer introduced using magnetic tape for reprogramming, rather than rewiring required by previous models.

1950

Floppy disk is invented; computer pioneer Alan Turing predicts that a machine could someday duplicate human intelligence.

1951

Whirlwind, the first real-time computer, is built for the U.S. Air Defense System; UNIVAC-1, the first commercial, general-purpose computer, is delivered to U.S. Bureau of Census.

1953

Total number of computers in the world is estimated at one hundred; Magnetic Core Memory developed.

1956

First conference on artificial intelligence is held at Dartmouth College in New Hampshire.

1957

IBM markets first dot matrix printer; FORTRAN (FORmula TRANslation), a programming language used for science, is developed; the editor of business books for Prentice-Hall says, "I have traveled the length and breadth of this country and talked with the best people, and I can assure you that data processing is a fad that won't last out the year."

1958

Jack St. Clair Kilby of Texas Instruments invents the integrated circuit.

1959

COBOL (COmmon Business-Oriented Language) is developed; smaller computers, based on transistors and printed circuits and able to handle both FORTRAN for science and COBOL for business, are produced.

1964

Even smaller IBM computers, based on integrated circuits, are developed and sold to businesses; Digital Equipment Corporation builds the first minicomputer, available for $16,000.

1965

BASIC (Beginner's All-purpose Symbolic Instruction Code) is developed, later used to teach programming; the mouse is developed, becoming popular with Apple in 1983 and IBM in 1987; Control Data develops the first supercomputer; Intel cofounder Gordon Moore predicts that chip speeds will double every 18–20 months, a rule that becomes known as Moore's law.

1968
Gordon Moore, Robert Noyce, and friends found Intel; LOGO programming language is developed.

1969
ARPANET, the original basis of what now forms the Internet, is established by the U.S. Department of Defense for research into networking; Al Gore first calls the growing network the Information Superhighway.

1970
Intel introduces the first RAM chip with a capacity of 1 K-bit, 1,024 bits; introduction of UNIX operating system, still widely used in network and Internet servers; FORTH programming language developed; flight data processor for the U.S. Navy Tomcat fighter jet is developed.

1971
Intel develops and releases the first microprocessor; PASCAL programming language is developed.

1972
Nolan Bushnell founds Atari; Pong, the first arcade video game, is released; modern computers, based on LSI (large scale integration) of circuits such as microprocessors with five hundred or more components on a chip, is built (today's circuits have millions of components); C programming language is developed; Hewlett-Packard releases the first handheld scientific calculator; first international connections to ARPANET are established.

1973
Prolog, a language often used for AI programming, is developed; Ethernet, a way of connecting PCs and other computers to share data and printers, is developed.

1975
Intel introduces 8080, an 8-bit microprocessor; MIT's Altair 8800, the first personal computer commercially available, is released; *Popular Mechanics* advertises for $397 kits for the computer, based on Intel's 8080.

1975
Bill Gates and Paul Allen first implement BASIC for MIT's Altair and form Microsoft; IBM releases 5100.

1976
Steve Wozniak and Stephen Jobs found Apple Computer to market Apple I; IBM introduces the first laser printer; Zilog releases Z80, the basis for the computer boom in the early 1980s; the 8-bit microprocessor 6502 is developed and chosen to equip Apple II, Acorn, BBC Micro, Commodore 64, and Commodore PET; Cray 1, the first commercial supercomputer containing 200,000 freon-cooled integrated circuits, is developed.

1977
Ken Olson, founder of Digital Equipment Corporation, says, "There is no reason anyone would want a computer in their home"; Apple II is introduced.

1978
Arcade video game "Space Invaders" is released.

1979
Commodore PET is released with 8K RAM, cassette deck, and 9-inch monitor; the compact disc (CD) is invented; IBM commissions Microsoft to write the operating system for a new personal computer.

1981
Xerox 8010 ("Star") system is introduced, the first system to use WIMP (windows, icons, menus, and pointing devices), which Apple uses for the Macintosh and Microsoft uses for Windows; IBM PC is available, the standard model selling for $2,880, with additional options available; all IBM PC–compatible computers use the MS-DOS operating system; Pacman is written.

1982
Commodore 64 is released; Compaq releases the Compaq Portable; MIDI (Musical Instrument Digital Interface) is published, a system that allows computers to be connected to instruments like keyboards; Sony and Philips introduce audio CDs; Sinclair ZQ Spectrum is released with 8-color graphics; IBM launches the double-sided 320K floppy disk drive.

1983
IBM XT is released with MS-DOS 2.0; MS-DOS 2.25, with foreign-language character sets, is sold in the Far East.

1984
Hewlett-Packard releases laserjet printer; Apple releases the Macintosh.

1985
Sony produces CD-ROM; MS-DOS 3.1, the first version to provide network support, is released; Microsoft Windows, still requiring DOS, is launched.

1986
Apple releases Macintosh Plus; Sinclair ZX Spectrum 128 is released; Apple releases Macintosh 512Ke; Amstrad releases Amstrad PC 1512 at a cost of just under $1,000.

1987
Connection Machine, a supercomputer using microprocessors, performs 2 billion operations per second; Macintosh II, fitted with a color video adapter, is released; IBM introduces PS/2 system and VGA, designed for PS/2; AD-LIB soundcard is released.

1988
First optical chip developed, using light instead of electricity to increase processing speed; IBM markets WORM (Write Once Read Many times); Common Access Method (CAM) committee is formed.

1989
World Wide Web invented as information exchange for physicists; Sony and Philips release CD-I; Intel releases 80486 DX, containing about 1.2 million transistors; Macintosh releases the portable; Creative Labs releases Sound Blaster Card, compatible with AD-LIB soundcard of 1987.

1990
Bill Gates and Microsoft introduce Windows 3.0, containing a multitask system; Macintosh Classic and Macintosh IIsi are released with a 256-color video adapter.

1991
Collaboration between Microsoft and IBM on DOS ends; Linux, a free operating system, is born.

1992
Philips launches CD-I; Sound Blaster 16 ASP is introduced.

1993
Commercial providers allowed to sell Internet connections to individuals, the beginning of an explosion in Internet use; Intel releases Pentium with over 3.1 million transistors.

1994
Linus Torvalds releases version 1.0 of Linux Kernel; Doom II, a platform making games such as "Theme Park" and "Magic Carpet" available on PCs, is released.

1995
Linux '95 released; Intel releases the 120 and 133 MHz versions of Pentium processor; Bill Gates and Microsoft release Windows '95, a system not reliant on DOS; CompuServe blocks access to 200 sexually explicit sites, all but 5 restored in February 1996; Netscape develops JavaScript; RISC processor used in PCs.

1996
Netscape Navigator 2.0, the first browser to support JavaScript, released; Intel releases new versions of Pentium processor, which contain over 3.3 million transistors; Linux 2.0 released.

1997
Intel releases Pentium MMX for games and multimedia enhancement; IBM's Deep Blue computer beats world chess champion Gary Kasparov; Microsoft invests in Apple, buying 100,000 non-voting shares, and Apple temporarily drops its court case against Microsoft for copying Apple's operating system for Windows.

1998
Microsoft releases Windows '98.

1999
Linux 2.20 released; Apple releases PowerMac G4.

2000
U.S. government relaxes restrictions on exporting cryptography, thus no longer requiring U.S. companies to create U.S. and international copies of software; Transmeta, in competition with Intel, launches the "Crusoe" chips for laptops; Microsoft releases Windows 2000.

2001
Linux 2.40 released; Apple releases MacOS X; Microsoft releases the "X" Box, the games console and system to connect to the Internet for multiplayer game.

For Further Research

Books

Sara Baase, *A Gift of Fire: Social, Legal, and Ethical Issues in Computing.* Upper Saddle River, NJ: Prentice-Hall, 1997.

Vincente Berdages and John W. Murphy, *Computers, Human Interaction, and Organizations.* Westport, CT: Praeger, 2000.

Tim Berness-Lee with Mark Fischetti, *Weaving the Web: The Original Design and Ultimate Destiny of the World Wide Web by Its Inventor.* New York: HarperCollins, 1999.

J. David Bolter, *Turing's Man: Western Culture in the Computer Age.* Chapel Hill: University of North Carolina Press, 1984.

Stacey L. Edgar, *Morality and Machines: Perspectives on Computer Ethics.* Sudbury, MA: Joans and Bartlett, 1997.

Marc Eisenstadt and Tom Vincent, *The Knowledge Web: Learning and Collaborating on the Net.* London: Kogan Page, 1998.

Bill Gates with Collins Hemingway, *Business @ the Speed of Thought: Using a Digital Nervous System.* New York: Warner Books, 1999.

Jan L. Harrington, *Ethernet Networking Clearly Explained.* San Diego: Academic Press, 1999.

Michael Hiltzik, *Dealers of Lightning: Xerox PARC and the Dawn of the Computer Age.* New York: HarperCollins, 1999.

Tim Jackson, *Inside Intel: Andy Grove and the Rise of the World's Most Powerful Chip Company.* New York: Dutton, 1997.

Stephen Johnson, *Interface Culture: How New Technology Transforms the Way We Create and Communicate.* New York: HarperCollins, 1997.

Martha E. Kendall, *Steve Wozniak: Inventor of the Apple Computer.* New York: Walker, 1994.

Rob Kling, ed., *Computerization and Controversy: Value Conflicts and Social Choices.* 2nd ed. San Diego: Academic Press, 1996.

Jacqueline Klosek, *Data Privacy in the Information Age.* Westport, CT: Quorum Books, 2000.

Michael Lewis, *The New New Thing: A Silicon Valley Story.* New York: W.W. Norton, 2000.

Fred Moody, *The Visionary Position: The Inside Story of the Digital Dreamers Who Are Making Virtual Reality a Reality.* New York: Random House, 1999.

Janet H. Murray, *Hamlet on the Holodeck: The Future of Narrative in Cyberspace.* New York: Free Press, 1997.

John G. Nellist and Elliott M. Gilbert, *Understanding Modern Telecommunication and the Information Superhighway.* Boston: Artech House, 1999.

Mary Northrup, *American Computer Pioneers.* Springfield, NJ: Enslow, 1998.

Ian Pearson and Chris Winter, *Where's IT Going?* New York: Thames & Hudson, 1999.

Gregory J.E. Rawlins, *Moths to the Flame: The Seductions of Computer Technology.* Cambridge, MA: MIT Press, 1996.

Douglas S. Robertson, *The New Renaissance: Computers and the Next Level of Civilization.* New York: Oxford University Press, 1998.

Gene I. Rochlin, *Trapped in the Net: The Unanticipated Consequences of Computerization.* Princeton, NJ: Princeton University Press, 1997.

Stephen Segaller, *Nerds 2.0.1: A Brief History of the Internet.* New York: TV Books, 1998.

Richard J. Severson, *The Principles of Information Ethics.* New York: M.E. Sharpe, 1997.

Robert Slater, *Saving Big Blue: Leadership Lessons and Turnaround Tactics of IBM's Lou Gerstner.* New York: McGraw-Hill, 1999.

Kara Swisher, *aol.com: How Steve Case Beat Bill Gates, Nailed the Netheads, and Made Millions in the War for the Web.* New York: Times Books, 1998.

Periodicals

Gary H. Anthes, "Internet to Mars," *Computerworld*, July 16, 2001.

Gregory Beals, "The Future of Computers," *Newsweek International*, June 18, 2001.

Judith Berck, "Digital Tethers, Digital Freedom (The Wired Retirement Home)," *New York Times*, April 5, 2001.

Business Week, "Sorry, but the New Economy Demands New Regulations," July 30, 2001.

Sean Captain, "Stealth Surfing," *PC World*, August 2001.

Margaret Carlson, "Someone to Watch Over Me: How to Tell the Good Surveillance from the Bad," *Time*, July 16, 2001.

Computer Weekly, "Online Archive Shows the Life of Alan Turing," January 18, 2001.

Jennifer DiSabatino, "Tracking Your Every Move," *Computerworld*, May 21, 2001.

John C. Dvorak, "Net Addiction," *PC/Computing*, June 1997.

Anita Hamilton, "Let's Chat About Books: Online Discussion Groups Can Keep You Turning the Pages—Once You Find a Club That Fits," *Time*, August 6, 2001.

Dana Hawkins, "Gospel of Privacy Guru: Be Wary; Assume the Worst," *U.S. News & World Report*, June 25, 2001.

Thomas Hayden and Peter Hadfield, "The Age of Robots," *U.S. News & World Report*, April 23, 2001.

Luis Ramiro Hernandez, "Integrated Risk Management in the Internet Age," *Risk Management*, June 2000.

Kurt Kleiner, "Free Speech, Liberty, Pornography," *New Scientist*, March 10, 2001.

Lynne Lamberg, "Confidentiality and Privacy of Electronic Medical Records: Psychiatrists Explore Risks of the 'Information Age,'" *JAMA*, June 27, 2001.

Newsweek, "New Technology Will Help You Monitor Your Health, Treat Your Phobias, Screen Your Blood, Check Your Moles and Scope Out Your System," June 25, 2001.

Stephen Nickson and Jim Kates, "The Reality of Hackers," *Risk Management*, July 2001.

David Noonan, "Surgery of the Future: The Ultimate Remote Control," *Newsweek*, June 25, 2001.

Robin Rasken, "Funding E-Learning," *Family PC*, August 2000.

Patrick Thibodeau, "Cybersecurity Legislation Nears with CIA Testimony," *Computerworld*, June 25, 2001.

Bryant Urstadt, "Big PC on Campus," *Family PC*, August 2001.

Index

About the Editor

After many years of teaching British literature to high school students, Clarice Swisher now devotes her time to research and writing. She is the author of *The Age of Monarchs, Albert Einstein, Pablo Picasso, Genetic Engineering, Victorian England, The Glorious Revolution,* and editor of *The Spread of Islam* and *Galileo*. She is currently working on a new series, *Understanding Great Literature*. She lives in St. Paul, Minnesota.